OSCE Insights

Cornelius Friesendorf | Argyro Kartsonaki (Eds.)

OSCE Insights 2022

War in Europe

The Deutsche Nationalbibliothek lists this publication in the Deutsche Nationalbibliografie; detailed bibliographic data are available on the Internet at http://dnb.d-nb.de

ISBN 978-3-8487-7512-5 (Print)
978-3-7489-3362-5 (ePDF)

British Library Cataloguing-in-Publication Data
A catalogue record for this book is available from the British Library.

ISBN 978-3-8487-7512-5 (Print)
978-3-7489-3362-5 (ePDF)

Library of Congress Cataloging-in-Publication Data
Friesendorf, Cornelius | Kartsonaki, Argyro
OSCE Insights 2022
War in Europe
Cornelius Friesendorf | Argyro Kartsonaki (Eds.)
80 pp.
Includes bibliographic references.

ISBN 978-3-8487-7512-5 (Print)
978-3-7489-3362-5 (ePDF)

1st Edition 2023

Published by
Nomos Verlagsgesellschaft mbH & Co. KG
Waldseestraße 3–5 | 76530 Baden-Baden
www.nomos.de

Production of the printed version:
Nomos Verlagsgesellschaft mbH & Co. KG
Waldseestraße 3–5 | 76530 Baden-Baden

ISBN (Print): 978-3-8487-7512-5
ISBN (ePDF): 978-3-7489-3362-5

DOI: https://doi.org/10.5771/9783748933625

Onlineversion
Nomos eLibrary

Contents

Introduction to *OSCE Insights* 2022: War in Europe

Cornelius Friesendorf and Argyro Kartsonaki[*]

To cite this publication: Cornelius Friesendorf and Argyro Kartsonaki, "Introduction to *OSCE Insights* 2022: War in Europe," in *OSCE Insights*, eds. Cornelius Friesendorf and Argyro Kartsonaki (Baden-Baden: Nomos, 2023), https://doi.org/10.5771/9783748933625-00

The OSCE has never been a fair-weather organization, but 2022 was one of its worst years yet. Vladimir Putin's decision to order a full-scale attack on Ukraine and Russia's brutal conduct of the war violated international law and fundamental OSCE principles. Russia's war raises the question of how a consensus-based organization can deal with a major state that no longer respects the basic rules.

The weakening of the OSCE has also shown itself in the participating States' failure to agree on matters vital to keeping the Organization operational, including the budget. Throughout 2022, the OSCE was operating on monthly provisional allotments, making strategic planning impossible. Moreover, due to high inflation and unfavorable exchange rates, it was running short of money, which hindered the continuation of some of its activities.

Russia's veto forced the OSCE to close its field operations in Ukraine, and many worried that other operations would follow suit. Agreement on extending the mandates of the field operations eventually came in late 2022, but no agreement was reached on who would chair the OSCE in 2024. The Ministerial Council in Łódź in December 2022 did not yield any results. Rather, the Polish Chair's decision not to grant a visa to Russian Foreign Minister Sergei Lavrov, and Moscow's indignant response, revealed how difficult it has become to even sit in the same room.

Not all problems in the OSCE were directly about Russia, though. Unrest in Kazakhstan resulted in casualties and a military intervention. There was renewed fighting between Armenia and Azerbaijan, and both states stymied agreement on the 2022 budget, as they had done in previous years. Kyrgyzstan and Tajikistan engaged in armed clashes, and bloodshed marked public protests during a constitutional crisis in the Uzbek autonomous region of Karakalpakstan.

* Cornelius Friesendorf
Institute for Peace Research and Security Policy at the University of Hamburg (IFSH), friesendorf@ifsh.de

Argyro Kartsonaki
Institute for Peace Research and Security Policy at the University of Hamburg (IFSH), kartsonaki@ifsh.de

Nonetheless, the core issue was the antagonism between a revisionist Russia and NATO/EU members. The vitality of the OSCE has always mirrored Western-Russian relations, and thus it is no surprise that the very survival of the OSCE was at stake in 2022, at a time when NATO states and Russia risked being drawn into direct conflict.

At the same time, 2022 also demonstrated the OSCE's resilience. States with an interest in maintaining the OSCE, together with the Secretariat, flexibly dealt with decision blockades to keep the OSCE operational. Voluntary financial contributions became more important, and a group of participating States launched a new multi-year program for Ukraine (the Support Programme for Ukraine). The OSCE continued its work in many participating States. The extension of the field operations' mandates in December 2022 shows that consensus is even possible in the shadow of a major war in Europe. Thus, all in all, the OSCE's chances of withstanding the systemic shock of Russia's war looked much better in late 2022 than they had in the weeks immediately following February 24, 2022.

Against this backdrop, the authors of the 2022 edition of *OSCE Insights* discuss three questions: (1) Can the OSCE still offer value to participating States and societies? (2) How can governments deal with Russia within the OSCE? (3) How can the OSCE be preserved and its vitality increased? Answering these questions is challenging; Russia's attack on Ukraine is ongoing, and the outcome of the war will inevitably affect the role of the OSCE in any post-war European security order. In the following, we provide a summary of our contributors' main responses to these three questions.

Can the OSCE still offer value to participating States and societies?

The contributors to this volume agree that the OSCE is under severe pressure. While the main focus is the war against Ukraine, the policy briefs also illustrate a broader trend: participating States' preferences have increasingly diverged since the CSCE became the OSCE in the 1990s.

Nonetheless, despite the erosion of normative consensus within the OSCE area, the contributors to this volume argue that the OSCE can still offer value to governments and societies. William Hill and Jelena Cupać stress the forum function of the OSCE. The OSCE may become less relevant as an actor in its own right but will nevertheless remain important because it is a "logical venue" (Hill) for dialogue on pan-European security issues, including military confidence- and security-building measures. Forums also allow states to signal their interests; thus, Western states could signal to Russia that they are not ready to negotiate zones of influence and that they will not compromise on core OSCE principles (see Cupać's contribution).

Andrei Zagorski reminds us that the CSCE process would have ended if states had not been able to agree on follow-up meetings—and indeed, it nearly did end several times. Yet the OSCE is more institutionalized than the CSCE was. This reminder cautions against pursuing initiatives that would result in the OSCE's reverting to a CSCE-style conference cycle.

Walter Kemp offers another historical reminder. Pointing out that the planning for the creation of the United Nations took place in the midst of World War II, he argues that the OSCE should devise a plan for stability in Europe even though the war against Ukraine is ongoing. Kemp suggests that while the outcome of the war will certainly impact any such plan, the OSCE ought to develop a strategy for if and when negotiations on a new European security order commence.

Creativity and compromises are not necessarily beneficial to all, however. In his analysis of OSCE activities in Turkmenistan, Luca Anceschi writes that "Turkmen-OSCE relations are marked by a minimum level of engagement and the avoidance of discussing thorny co-operation issues concerning human rights and good governance promotion." Focusing on the activities of the OSCE Centre in Ashgabat and on ODIHR election observation efforts amid restrictions imposed by the Turkmen government, Anceschi reveals that what may be good for a participating State does not automatically benefit that state's society. His paper identifies a fundamental dilemma faced by the OSCE: How can a human rights–based organization meaningfully engage with authoritarian states that are part of that organization?

How can governments deal with Russia within the OSCE?

After February 24, 2022, many within the OSCE contemplated whether and how to suspend Russia's participation in the Organization. The contributors to this volume who discuss this question recommend keeping Russia in. For William Hill, an OSCE without Russia would not only lose its relevance but would turn Russia into a "perpetual disruptor." Keeping Russia (and smaller states that block consensus) in the OSCE may make it more difficult to reach agreement, "but diplomacy on hard, contested issues is never easy." Hill argues that the history of the CSCE suggests that at some point, Western states "will find it possible and desirable to engage seriously and substantively with Russia once again."

For Wolfgang Zellner, Russia's suspension would be formally justified on the basis of the suspension of Yugoslavia from 1992 to 2000. Practically, however, securing its suspension would be problematic insofar as Belarus and other members of the Collective Security Treaty Organization (CSTO) are unlikely to vote Russia out. It is equally doubtful that Russia would leave the OSCE on its own initiative, as other CSTO members would likely remain, thus exposing its isolation. Zellner recommends continuing dialogue on European security with Russia if possible. He argues that while states should call out Russia's violations of OSCE principles, symbolic actions such as walk-outs are counter-productive.

The question of how to balance isolating and engaging Russia is a difficult one, however, and our authors' answers vary. Mette Eilstrup-Sangiovanni cautions that there may come a time when Russia feels compelled to leave the OSCE. A potential parallel is Germany's leaving the League of Nations in 1933. Andrei Zagorski reminds us that, in contrast to the USSR's engagement in the CSCE, Russia no longer regards the OSCE as a primary venue for discussing European security with Western states.

Eilstrup-Sangiovanni, Zagorski, and Cupać also recommend that states avoid confrontation over issues on which there is little room for compromise, in particular democratization. This does not mean that Western states should abandon liberal norms—in fact, Western states should reaffirm these norms. However, they should refrain from blaming and shaming (which, as Andrei Zagorski reminds us, almost ended the CSCE process). Instead, the OSCE could serve as a forum for de-escalating tension and identifying issues of common interest. Such efforts would have to be led by states rather than executive structures. Walter Kemp's paper notes that, in his attempt to find common ground among participating States, former Secretary General Thomas Greminger was accused of being too close to Moscow—a reaction that illustrates the limited autonomy granted by governments to the OSCE Secretariat.

How can the OSCE be preserved and its vitality increased?

As a central question cutting across all contributions, the authors explore whether and how the OSCE might not only overcome Russia's war against Ukraine but become a more important pillar of pan-European security. William Hill offers suggestions for how states can make best use of the OSCE's forum function. In this regard, he calls for less "political posturing and public relations" in order to make room for meaningful dialogue. He also sees a potential role for the OSCE in Ukraine, for example by contributing to a future ceasefire or peace agreement. In addition to the outcome of the war, however, the OSCE's ability to play a role will depend on NATO and EU member states' bringing important issues to the OSCE. Hill is also less optimistic about the future of structures and institutions such as ODIHR, whose budgets and size are likely to shrink due to a lack of consensus. As he argues, "we will face a prolonged period in which many important OSCE documents and commitments will be honored more in the breach than the (rigorous) observance."

Similarly, Wolfgang Zellner argues that the future of the OSCE depends on how participating States use the Organization. He proposes an interim strategy that maximizes the OSCE's options. The strategy relies on informal arrangements in case of Russian vetoes, including the use of extrabudgetary contributions to fund OSCE institutions. In addition, he suggests that the OSCE should engage states in areas where Russian influence is waning and where there is a high risk of conflict, in particular the South Caucasus and Central Asia. According to Zellner, however, a more informal, flexible OSCE depends on significant political will and intense consultations, and thus on giving a strong role to the Chairperson-in-Office and the Troika.

Two of our authors draw on lessons from the past. Mette Eilstrup-Sangiovanni reveals coping strategies used by the League of Nations, arguing that the OSCE can learn from both its failures and its successes. As she observes, the League should not be regarded as a failure given that many of its activities live on in the United Nations. She stresses that the crisis faced by the OSCE is political and that institutional reform (such as improving the budget process) is therefore of limited utility. Instead, she recommends exploiting a flexible mandate: the OSCE should avoid getting bogged down in debates on contentious issues such as human rights and arms control and should instead focus on areas where there is potential for consensus, such as economic connectivity and the security implications of climate change. Another lesson from the League is the importance of broadening political support. Arguing that a large, heterogeneous membership helps international organizations to survive, she recommends that the OSCE engage states that have not been very active thus far, such as Central Asian states (mirroring Wolfgang Zellner's recommendation). She suggests further that the OSCE should work towards receiving more support from external actors such as NGOs, which have significant technical expertise.

Andrei Zagorski shows how we can learn from the CSCE. The Soviet Union and the United States at times considered withdrawing from the CSCE and used meetings for blaming and shaming. The Soviet Union's reservations about the West's focus on human rights is similar to Russia's criticism of its current emphasis on the human dimension. But the CSCE survived thanks to what Zagorski calls "asymmetric bargaining," which reflected the divergent interests of participating States and created a setting in which "balanced progress" could be made across the different baskets. The history of the CSCE also suggests that states could use the OSCE as a forum for clarifying ambiguous principles such as non-intervention in internal affairs. Zagorski argues that the applicability of these lessons depends on the outcome of the current crisis. If the situation allows, an agreement on common rules could underpin a modus vivendi.

Drawing on his experience as head of the OSCE Strategic Policy Support Unit, Walter Kemp calls on the OSCE to develop a strategy for returning to co-operative security. As Kemp argues, the development of a strategy would not require consensus; it could be informal and include external experts. It would, however, require leadership by the Troika. Key elements of a co-operative security agenda include arms control and confidence- and security-building measures. In this sense, Kemp departs from Mette Eilstrup-Sangiovanni, who recommends avoiding divisive issues as far as possible. Like Eilstrup-Sangiovanni, though, Kemp proposes that the OSCE should also consider issues that have thus far been excluded from the OSCE's core agenda, such as the security implications of climate change. He lists various innovations made during his tenure but also reveals how participating States restrict the autonomy of the Secretariat.

For Luca Anceschi, the OSCE's engagement with Turkmenistan has been inadequate. He argues that minimal and selective engagement reduces the OSCE's relevance insofar as it limits change to those areas in which the OSCE operates. This also undermines security in the OSCE area since authoritarian politics, he argues, is a source of insecurity. As an alternative, he proposes that the OSCE's engagement with Turkmenistan should treat authoritarian politics as a problem. Consequently, the OSCE should refrain from activities such as election observation under restrictive conditions and, more systematically, should promote human rights.

In sum, the contributions to *OSCE Insights* 2022 present perspectives and recommendations that could help the OSCE not only to survive but to become a more vital contributor to co-operative and comprehensive security.

Acknowledgements

We are grateful to the authors for sharing their ideas on how the OSCE can cope with seemingly intractable problems. We also thank the reviewers for taking the time to comment on draft papers and our colleagues from the Institute for Peace Research and Security Policy at the University of Hamburg (IFSH) and from IFSH's Centre for OSCE Research (CORE). We are particularly grateful to André Härtel and our Russian-speaking co-ordinator for managing the production of the German- and Russian-language editions of *OSCE Insights*, respectively. Our deepest thanks go to Frank Evers for providing OSCE expertise and for his tireless co-ordination of CORE's complex workflows.

Also crucial were our editors, translators, and proofreaders, who worked thoroughly and patiently. We thank Corina Alt, Carolyn Benson, Roman Dobrokhotov, Olena Sivuda, and Michael Weh. We also benefited from the support of Stefan Wolff and Andrei Zagorski. The German Federal Foreign Office provided funding, and the contributors to this volume received helpful information from various foreign ministries and OSCE executive structures and institutions (the views expressed in this volume are those of the authors alone). Last but not least, we thank Nomos Publishing, especially Eva Lang and Carsten Rehbein, for sharing our enthusiasm about *OSCE Insights*.

The OSCE Approaching Fifty: Does the Organization Have a Future?

William H. Hill[*] [1]

Abstract

Russia's invasion of Ukraine has raised questions about the future of the OSCE: How can any institution dedicated to co-operation and security include the Russian Federation? Despite such doubts, the OSCE can have a future, though one that is more modest and contentious. The post-2022 OSCE should provide a pan-European venue for dialogue on important security issues, similar to its original function in the 1970s. OSCE institutions established after the Cold War will be less active, reflecting the pronounced lack of consensus among participating States. OSCE norms such as the Final Act's ten principles do not need to be renegotiated but should remain ideals toward which all participating States aspire. There are fundamental security issues affecting Europe which desperately need to be addressed. The OSCE will survive if participating States make it the forum in which to seek and find agreement on these issues.

Keywords

OSCE, security, Russia, pan-European

To cite this publication: William H. Hill, "The OSCE Approaching Fifty: Does the Organization Have a Future?," in *OSCE Insights*, eds. Cornelius Friesendorf and Argyro Kartsonaki (Baden-Baden: Nomos, 2023), https://doi.org/10.5771/9783748933625-01

Introduction

In late 2021, the question in the title of this paper might have seemed outlandish, as many European diplomats were pondering whether and where to hold a summit in 2025 to mark the fiftieth anniversary of the adoption of the Helsinki Final Act. Now, in light of Russia's unprovoked attack on and war with Ukraine, many of these same diplomats wonder how any institution dedicated to security and co-operation can include the Russian Federation as a member.

Well into the fifth decade of the Helsinki process, Russia's massive assault on Ukraine has violated many if not most of the principles adopted in Helsinki in 1975 and strengthened, deepened, and broadened in the 1990 Charter of Paris and a number of other landmark OSCE normative documents. In particular, Moscow's attack on Kiev violates—at least—OSCE commitments on refraining from the use of force, inviolability of borders, territorial integrity of states,

* William H. Hill
Global Fellow
Wilson Center, Washington DC

peaceful settlement of disputes, and the Final Act's fundamental commitment to peace, security, and justice. There have been wars between OSCE participating States before, in particular in the Balkans and the South Caucasus in the 1990s. However, there has not been a war of this scope between two of the largest states in Europe since World War II, and certainly never in the half-century history of the CSCE/OSCE.

The United States may be especially wary of re-engaging with Russia after the war, whether in the OSCE or elsewhere. While some American diplomats highly value the OSCE, the Organization has never been particularly popular, well known, or well understood by US political leaders and the American voting public. For most, the OSCE is known as a relatively obscure European human rights organization, if at all. Against this background, a number of US officials are already asking why it makes sense to support a human rights institution with Russia in it when Moscow is violating most of its commitments to it. At best, some suggest keeping the OSCE but kicking Russia out. That idea is probably a non-starter, as discussion below will show. However, such sentiments suggest a bleak future for an organization whose aims include fostering co-operation between the United States and Russia.

If the OSCE is to survive Russia's war against Ukraine, participating States will need to return the Organization to its original purpose: political and security dialogue between opposing, often hostile states. Political leaders must recognize that OSCE institutions and operations born and sustained by the unusually broad consensus at the end of the Cold War will not enjoy that level of support and will likely be less active after Russia's invasion of Ukraine. Basic OSCE norms and commitments need not be renegotiated, but participating States must reconcile themselves to an international environment in which many are violated, frequently and at times severely. Despite such impediments, there are key political and security issues of pan-European interest which urgently need to be addressed. The OSCE is the logical venue to do so.

This paper aims to understand how the OSCE's current structure and operations came to be in order to determine how it might survive in a post–Ukraine war future. The narrative examines the purpose of the Cold War CSCE and the establishment of its institutions and operations when the Cold War ended. The text then reviews the debate over the European security architecture in the 1990s and how this affected the role of the OSCE and Russia's attitude toward the Organization. Finally, the paper analyzes the current structure and operations of the OSCE, the security situation in Europe, and what issues and tasks the future OSCE might address.

Why did the CSCE/OSCE come into being?

To envision what the OSCE might be like after the war in Ukraine, I find it useful to begin by recalling why the CSCE came into being in the first place. In the early 1970s, the United States, the Soviet Union, and the major European powers were all interested in pursuing critical security and political aims through an all-Europe multilateral negotiation. Since the early 1950s, the USSR had been proposing a European security conference to sign a peace treaty which would formally acknowledge the territorial changes in Europe that had been agreed at Yalta in February 1945. The United States and its allies initially resisted these Soviet proposals, but by the late 1960s Washington evinced an increasing desire for the "normalization" of East-West relations, which would include strategic and conventional arms control and broad agreement on conduct between, but also within, states (in particular expansion of human contacts and observance of human rights).

The aspirations for a broad East-West agreement led to not only the Final Act and the subsequent "Helsinki process," but also the Mutual and Balanced Force Reductions conventional arms negotiations, ultimately culminating in the 1990 Conventional Armed Forces in Europe Treaty (CFE). From the very beginning, the CSCE—or Helsinki process—was both normative and operational. The follow-up and interim experts' meetings continued to discuss and expand commitments in all three baskets, fashioning specific norms and commitments for inter-state and intra-state conduct. The confidence- and security-building measures (CSBMs) in the Final Act required a modicum of contacts, observation, and reporting, which grew over time as the CSBMs were expanded in subsequent negotiations.

The crucial point in this overly simplified review of the OSCE's beginnings is that all of the major OSCE participating States saw the institution—at that time an ongoing negotiating forum—as a venue in which they could pursue and attain some of their most important pan-European security, diplomatic, and political aims. This was certainly the case when the Final Act was signed in August 1975. I would argue that this continued to be the case at least through the adoption of the Charter of Paris and the CFE Treaty in November 1990, and perhaps the July 1992 Helsinki CSCE Summit and the adoption of the document Challenges of Change.

The CSCE and the end of the Cold War

The end of the Cold War brought a remarkable but brief degree of consensus among the CSCE participating States, which facilitated norm-setting activities. This unprecedented agreement among the participating States also shifted the balance in the emerging Organization toward operations. An Office for Free Elections established at the Paris Summit rapidly expanded to become ODIHR, the Office for Democratic Institutions and Human Rights, with a far broader and more intrusive mandate. The Conflict Prevention Centre (CPC), which opened in Vienna in 1991, soon became the headquarters support office for OSCE field missions. The first of these were agreed and deployed in 1992; by 2000, there were nineteen of them. The 1992 Helsinki Summit established the High Commissioner on National Minorities (HCNM), whose quiet diplomacy and mediation quickly became highly valued throughout the OSCE space.

After 1990, the CSCE continued to be a forum for broad political and security dialogue, but this dialogue was institutionalized in a Permanent Council composed of the heads of delegations, meeting at least once a week. Initially, these debates were freewheeling and wide-ranging but gradually became more institutionalized and formulaic. For military security questions, a Forum for Security Co-operation was established, also with regular meetings in Vienna. By the mid-1990s, the CSCE was transformed into the Organization for Security and Co-operation in Europe (the OSCE), with its headquarters in Vienna.

The OSCE operations that proliferated so rapidly during the 1990s were in most cases responses to events rather than the product of a carefully organized master plan. Thus, the nature of field missions changed constantly during the 1990s and early 2000s, from conflict resolution to post-conflict rehabilitation to transition assistance. The Dutch proposal for the HCNM can be viewed as a response to growing ethnic and national animosities, exemplified by the wars in the former Yugoslavia in the 1990s. Thus, one might argue that these operations and activities reflect momentary agreement at various points in time rather than a lasting consensus on the purpose and primary activities of the OSCE.

OSCE operations, when added to the institution's continuing normative activity, constituted an enormous expansion of the scope and reach of the Organization. From 1975 through 1990, the participating States gradually allowed intrusion in their domestic affairs, initially by setting standards for how states should treat their own citizens, by pointing out how and when these standards had failed to be observed, and by offering good offices to assist in compliance with adopted norms. From the very beginning, the Helsinki process involved a limited relinquishment or diminution of national sovereignty by each participating State through the admission that other states have a legitimate right to observe and question their domestic behavior. With ODIHR election observation, visits by the HCNM and staff, and the activities of the field missions, this process of voluntarily limiting or sharing sovereignty expanded dramatically after 1990.

Initially, almost all of the participating States considered this process to be a good thing. During the 1990s, OSCE states generally welcomed election observers and supported field missions aimed at conflict prevention, mediation, or post-conflict reconciliation and reconstruction. This process of shared sovereignty was (and is) voluntary and co-operative. OSCE election observation and field missions are deployed and operate with the consent of the receiving state, but their activities can entail deep involvement in sometimes sensitive or controversial aspects of the host country's domestic affairs. At the outset, such operations were seen as helpful efforts to assist states in resolving problems, meeting commitments, or making the difficult transition from one political-economic system to another. However, some participating States—most notably Russia—gradually came to perceive many of these OSCE operations as tools for the geopolitical advantage of some other participating States.

The debate over the European security architecture

The early consensus that allowed for the adoption of the Charter of Paris, the Copenhagen Document, the Vienna Document, and the Challenges of Change was soon replaced by disagreement on important issues. Well before the emergence of today's confrontation between Russia and the US, NATO, and the EU, during the 1990s different visions of the European security architecture emerged between Moscow and its major Western interlocutors. To oversimplify considerably, Russian leaders wanted the OSCE to be the central security institution in Europe, governed by a small UN-type security council of the major powers, including the United States and Russia. The United States and most of the major European powers were prepared to have the OSCE assume important tasks but focused on either NATO or the EU (or both) as Europe's leading political and security actors.

This debate over Europe's security architecture and the role of the OSCE continued through most of the 1990s and culminated at the 1999 OSCE Istanbul Summit. Two landmark documents were adopted by the Heads of the participating States at Istanbul. First was the Charter for European Security, an ambitious, comprehensive document which reflected in part Russia's aspirations to establish and manage a hierarchy of European security institutions. Russia sought (unsuccessfully) to make use of provisions of this document in at least a couple of instances, and Moscow still berates Western partners for failing to observe important provisions in it. In particular, in 2021–2022, Russian Foreign Minister Lavrov was especially vocal in claiming that Western states had failed to observe provisions from this document on the equal security of states, maintaining that no participating State should enhance its security at the expense of others.[2]

The other major document adopted at Istanbul was the Adapted CFE Treaty (ACFE), which, like its predecessor, did not include all participating States but was negotiated and signed in the context of the OSCE. The Western signatories to the ACFE attached conditions for ratification involving the withdrawal of Russian troops from Georgia and Moldova. Western states maintain that Russia has not met these conditions, and the ACFE has not been fully ratified nor entered into force.

In general, during the 2000s, NATO and EU expansion, combined with other political, economic, and security developments and events, produced a situation in Europe in which key security and political issues were debated and decided increasingly in Brussels and Washington, and not anywhere near as often in Vienna. In my book *No Place for Russia*, I chronicle in much greater detail the growth and development of NATO and the EU and Moscow's increasing disillusionment with the OSCE after 2001–2002, all of which resulted in the Organization's growing difficulty in reaching consensus and producing significant results on important questions.[3] Russia in particular increasingly argued that many of the OSCE's operations relating to its domestic affairs, such as elections, were directed against it for the geopolitical benefit of certain other participating States.

Out of this process eventually emerged a Russia which is now alienated from most of its European partners, resentful, suspicious, uncooperative, and belligerent. Europe is once again divided between East and West, with the line of separation much further to the east than when the Cold War ended over thirty years ago. Even worse, there is a major war raging between Russia and its largest European neighbor. Whatever one may judge to be the causes of this situation, the major issue should be how to emerge from this crisis without an even broader war and how to reconstruct a European security system so that it does not happen again.

The present and future OSCE

This review of the OSCE's history provides several basic points which are essential both to understanding why the Organization is the way it is and to imagining what could make it relevant, useful, and desirable in the future. First, the Organization must provide a venue for real, substantive dialogue on essential security questions. It may also be used for political posturing and public relations, but if this becomes its primary purpose the Organization will die. If one or more participating States insist that the agenda should be restricted or exclude some issues, the Organization will die.

Second, membership must be universal, or else other institutions will have equal or better claims to relevance. Russia must remain a member; otherwise, the OSCE will be little better than a larger EU or NATO. As a perpetual outsider, Russia would be a perpetual disruptor. Including Russia (or obstinate smaller states) may make debates more contentious and reaching consensus more difficult, but diplomacy on hard, contested issues is never easy. The history of Belgrade's expulsion and readmittance to the OSCE is illustrative of the pitfalls of excluding a participating State. In 1992, it seemed only just to other Heads of State to banish Milosevic, but by 1997–1998 he felt he could ignore the OSCE, which by then greatly desired more leverage over him. Taking decisions without Russia may seem easier, but the point of the OSCE is to provide a forum for taking binding decisions *with* Russia.

Third, the Organization must be allowed to change as circumstances change. Many of the OSCE's institutions were built as responses to specific conditions and events. As circumstances alter and events proceed, some institutions will lose relevance or usefulness and should be allowed to wither or disappear. The Organization should continue, but many of its parts need not, at least in their present form.

Finally, the level of trust among the OSCE's participating States is at a historic low, with perhaps even greater mutual suspicion and animosity than existed in 1973 between the two superpowers and their alliances. In this sense, we are not just back to square one; we are arguably worse off. Before new universal norms can be agreed, before wide-ranging operations can be resumed, before full-scale co-operation can be initiated, a degree of mutual trust among participating States must be restored. The best way to do this would be to commence work on the most pressing issues that one can, in the hope that a process of open discussion, acceptance, and implementation of some decisions will assist a gradual restoration of mutual confidence. This process will be difficult, and one should not expect instant improvement or results.

After Russia's attack and all-out war on Ukraine, many Western leaders and international experts have found it hard to imagine an international organization dedicated to security and co-operation that includes the Russian Federation. Nevertheless, history suggests that at some point, perhaps sooner than many expect, states from Europe and North America will find it possible and desirable to engage seriously and substantively with Russia once again. In 1972, for example, less than four years after the Soviet suppression of the "Prague Spring," the United States and the USSR signed the Anti-Ballistic Missile Treaty and Strategic Arms Limitation Treaty. The multilateral negotiations which led to the Final Act began a year later. Notwithstanding the intense hostility that the Russian invasion of and war against Ukraine has aroused, it is still not out of the question to imagine how and when a broader political dialogue with Russia might resume.

What role might the OSCE play in this process? Given Russia's current violation of many of the most basic OSCE commitments adopted over the past four decades, can one reasonably expect the OSCE to play a role? The answer lies in the history of the Organization. The CSCE began as—and at its most fundamental level remains—a forum for political dialogue that includes all of the states of Europe, two major North American states, and the five former Soviet Central Asian states. So, if the OSCE will not be the venue for an eventual pan-European political dialogue that includes Russia, where will this dialogue take place? A review of the existing alternatives suggests that an institution that looks very much like the OSCE will have to be invented.

The OSCE's universal membership speaks in favor of maintaining the Organization. Rather than assuming that the OSCE can just pick up where it left off before the Russia-Ukraine war, however, we must recognize that the European security and political landscape in 2022 is very different from that faced by the diplomats who embarked on European security negotiations in Geneva in 1973. The aftermath of the war in Ukraine, irrespective of the arrangements that bring it to an end, will color attitudes toward Russia in ways quite different from how the Soviet Union was perceived in 1973. There are also structural and institutional changes in Europe that have fundamentally altered both how business is conducted within the OSCE and the range of issues that participating States will wish to bring to the OSCE.

From 1973 to 1990–1991, there were three basic groups of participating States within the OSCE: NATO, the Warsaw Pact, and the neutral and non-aligned states. These three groups would typically caucus to work out common positions on issues, which were then debated between the three groups in plenary sessions. Today both NATO and the EU include a much larger percentage of the participating States than before 1991. Their memberships also overlap significantly, although not entirely. The number of neutral and non-aligned states in the OSCE is much smaller than it once was. Furthermore, many of the neutrals aspire to EU (if not also NATO) membership and thus generally align themselves with EU positions. This means that when NATO or (especially) the EU adopts a position, it is very hard to resist or change it, given the de facto plurality of the EU. The number of participating States aligned with Russia is small, and Russia is almost always significantly outnumbered when either the EU or NATO has decided on a group position.

Finally, NATO and the EU sometimes simply take and implement decisions in which Russia believes it has an important interest without bringing them to the OSCE. Most egregiously, this occurred with the NATO decision to go to war against Serbia and Montenegro in March 1999 and the decision to recognize Kosovo's independence in 2008. Moscow was angered not only by the substance of these decisions but by the fact that NATO and the EU were able to take and implement them over the explicit, vocal opposition from Russia.

Given these structural features of the European security architecture and NATO and EU patterns of behavior, there has been increasingly less incentive for Moscow to bring important issues before the OSCE. Russian political leaders have increasingly portrayed the OSCE as a venue that their Western interlocutors use primarily to pressure or discredit Russia. It is easy to jump from this premise to the argument that Russia has a much better chance of influencing NATO and EU behavior by engaging early on in bilateral NATO-Russia or EU-Russia negotiations. The other path that may seem attractive to Moscow would be to attempt to split or disrupt the two blocs, an approach which has been increasingly evident over the past decade.

What can and should the OSCE do?

First of all, the OSCE can engage in what it was originally established to do—political dialogue on issues of interest to all the states of Europe. Such issues may be fewer in number or different from those that arose in 1973, but some do remain. Before its unprovoked attack on Ukraine on February 24, 2022, Russia raised some legitimate points for discussion among all of Europe's states amidst the two-month diplomatic barrage of otherwise unacceptable proposals to the United States, NATO, and the rest of Europe. Once the fighting has stopped in Ukraine and a reasonable settlement (even if only interim) is reached, OSCE participating States might resume discussion of some of these and other points.

Can the OSCE serve as a venue for negotiations to end the war in Ukraine? The OSCE is too large, unwieldy, and diverse to serve as a direct mediator in the conflict. That said, one or more participating States might reasonably offer themselves as mediators, with the negotiations to be held "in the context of the OSCE." Such an arrangement might enable interested participating States to be kept up to date on settlement progress and prospects and could provide for the use of OSCE institutions and resources in the implementation of any ceasefire or peace agreement.

From a broader and longer-term perspective, the OSCE can and should serve as a forum for serious discussion of conventional military security, especially questions related to confidence building and transparency. The latest Vienna Document (VDOC) and the ACFE are both based largely on conventional military weapons, equipment, and capabilities which are considerably outdated if not obsolete. The VDOC desperately needs to be updated, and discussions need to begin on how to build confidence and transparency in light of the composition and capabilities of present-day conventional militaries. Rules of the road and standards of conduct need to be established for new domains, capabilities, and challenges that simply did not exist when most of the OSCE's basic documents were adopted, for example cyber, social media, space, and climate change, to name just a few. Many of these issues will likely be addressed globally within the UN, but there still may be considerable room for discussion by the OSCE participating States of what might be agreed and done on a strictly regional basis.

Finally, there are the established structures and *acquis* of the OSCE—the CPC, field missions, ODIHR, the HCNM, the Representative on Freedom of the Media, and a host of important normative documents. These structures should not be abandoned, but participating States and individuals dedicated to the OSCE will need to admit and accept that, given the lack of consensus among the participating States, these institutions will almost certainly be less active and less ambitious. Their budgets and size will likely need to shrink. This is not to say that interested participating States should not try to employ missions and institutions to address pressing problems, but it will be much harder to obtain consensus for such efforts in the foreseeable future.

Similarly, we will face a prolonged period in which many important OSCE documents and commitments will be honored more in the breach than the (rigorous) observance. This need not be a disaster. The Universal Declaration of Human Rights has been egregiously violated by many states and leaders since it was first adopted in 1948 but still represents the landmark standard toward which we all aspire. The same should be the case with the Final Act, the Charter of Paris, and other landmark OSCE documents. These commitments and norms do not vanish simply because they have been violated; rather, we need to rededicate ourselves to their relevance and fulfillment.

The OSCE has an important anniversary coming up in 2025. In seeking to do something special for this jubilee, we do not need to revise the Helsinki Decalogue. Instead, an OSCE-wide endorsement of a Russia-Ukraine peace deal, along with security guarantees agreed and offered by select participating States, might include a rededication by all participating States to achieving better observance of OSCE principles. The Russia-Ukraine war and its aftermath are among the most critical security issues facing Europe today. By helping to address and resolve these issues, tasks that must be done somehow and somewhere, the OSCE might succeed in making itself important and relevant once again.

Notes

1 The author is a retired US Foreign Service Officer. He served twice as Head of the OSCE Mission to Moldova and as Co-ordinator for CSCE Affairs in the US Department of State. The opinions expressed are his own.

2 Reuters, "Russia cites 1999 charter text for insistence on 'indivisible security,'" February 1, 2022, https://www.reuters.com/world/europe/russia-cites-1999-charter-text-insistence-indivisible-security-2022-02-01/

3 William H. Hill, *No Place for Russia: European Security Institutions Since 1989* (New York: Columbia University Press, 2018).

Ending Up Somewhere Else: The Need for Strategy in the OSCE

Walter Kemp[*] [1]

Abstract

This paper examines past attempts to develop a strategy within the OSCE, their limited success, and their impact on the Organization. It also looks at how the war in Ukraine and tensions between Russia and the West have triggered a strategic rethink of security in Europe and what implications this could have for the Organization. The paper concludes that while it has been difficult for the OSCE to develop a strategy by design, it may have to develop a strategy by necessity—both to save itself and to restore peace and security in Europe.

Keywords
OSCE, strategy, Strategic Policy Support Unit, Ukraine, co-operative security

To cite this publication: Walter Kemp, "Ending Up Somewhere Else: The Need for Strategy in the OSCE," in *OSCE Insights*, eds. Cornelius Friesendorf and Argyro Kartsonaki (Baden-Baden: Nomos, 2023), https://doi.org/10.5771/9783748933625-02

Introduction

Strategy "bridges the gap from a less-desirable current state of affairs [...] to a more desirable future state of affairs."[2] Since its inception in 1975, the OSCE/CSCE has been all about moving Europe from a less desirable state of affairs to a more co-operative form of security. Generally speaking, a strategy identifies desired ends and figures out the ways, means, and capabilities that are needed to achieve the desired outcome. A strategy should also factor in the costs and risks of executing it. Within the OSCE there has not really been a strategy to guide the Organization towards achieving its goal of greater co-operative security.

When the Conference for Security and Co-operation in Europe (CSCE) was created in the early 1970s, there was a clear objective. As declared in the Helsinki Final Act, states participating in the CSCE wanted to promote better relations among themselves and ensure conditions in which their people could live in peace.[3] For the Communist bloc, the CSCE was a way of entrenching the status quo. For the West and Helsinki Committees (particularly in Eastern Europe) that were inspired by the human rights aspects of the Final Act, the CSCE was a way of promoting greater openness

* Director of the Strategy against Transnational Organized Crime at the Global Initiative and Strategic Policy Advisor at the Geneva Centre for Security Policy

behind the Iron Curtain, and even prying it open. Therefore, both sides—and neutral and non-aligned countries in between—had strategic interests in keeping the CSCE process going. The goal was to promote security through co-operation.

It worked. The CSCE contributed to managing East-West relations during the Cold War. Indeed, one could say that by 1989/90 the CSCE had achieved its goal. At the time, there was briefly talk that the CSCE could be the basis of a new common European home. While this did not win the support that President Gorbachev had hoped for, the Charter of Paris for a New Europe that was agreed on November 21, 1990, outlined a vision for a more united Europe and provided guidelines for the realization of a community of free and democratic states from Vancouver to Vladivostok. There was also a common understanding that reaching the lofty objectives of the Charter would "require a new quality of political dialogue and co-operation" and thus development of the structures of the CSCE.[4] Meetings became more regular and institutions were created, including a Secretariat, a Conflict Prevention Centre, an Office for Free Elections, and a Parliamentary Assembly. In short, there was a plan, and the CSCE was given the means (resources and capabilities) to achieve the desired ends.

However, the hope for a peaceful new era was dashed with conflicts in some parts of the former Soviet Union, including in Georgia and Moldova, and between Armenia and Azerbaijan. A new strategy was therefore needed to manage the challenges of change, and the CSCE needed new capabilities. These were developed creatively and quickly by appointing a High Commissioner on National Minorities, deploying field missions and creating permanent decision-making and governing bodies, establishing the post of Chairperson-in-Office, and strengthening early warning, conflict prevention, and crisis management capacities. The transformation from Conference to Organization was acknowledged with the change of name from CSCE to OSCE at the Budapest Summit of 1994.

However, by the time of the Budapest Summit, it was becoming evident that for some countries the priority was NATO and EU enlargement rather than making the OSCE the preeminent forum for dealing with European security. This led to increased tensions between Russia and the West which made it more difficult to co-operate. This worsening of relations made it all the more important to develop ways of enhancing common security but all the more difficult to agree on a common strategy.

This paper looks at attempts made to develop a strategy within the OSCE, focusing in particular on the Strategic Policy Support Unit (SPSU). The paper also explores the reasons why the OSCE has consistently failed to adopt a longer-term strategy, in contrast to other international organizations. It concludes with recommendations on how to develop a co-operative security agenda that would revive the OSCE and contribute to rebuilding the European security architecture.

Dialogue without strategy

One of the many quotations attributed to the American baseball player Yogi Berra is that "if you don't know where you are going, you will end up somewhere else." This certainly applies to the OSCE.

Since the mid-1990s there have been some successes in adopting strategies to address new global challenges, including the changing nature of security threats, terrorism, organized crime, violent extremism, hate crimes, and intra-state conflict. At the 1999 Istanbul Summit an effort was made to improve the security environment by adopting a Charter for European Security and an Agreement on Adaptation of the Treaty on Conventional Armed Forces in Europe. At the Ministerial Council in Maastricht in December 2003, participating States adopted an OSCE Strategy to Address Threats to Security and Stability in the Twenty-First Century and the OSCE Strategy Document for the Economic and Environmental Dimension. However, in the following years there was no attempt to look at how the OSCE's goals, mandates, and capacities could be applied systematically to deal with the challenges identified in those strategies.

While it had been possible to reach consensus on the strategic context, it was becoming more difficult to find common ground on how to deal with rapidly unfolding events. Color revolutions in Georgia and Ukraine, the war in Iraq, NATO enlargement, and the rise of a more assertive Russia under President Putin further strained relations between Russia and the West. In his speech at the Munich Security Conference in 2007, Putin criticized double standards, a breakdown of international law, NATO "expansion," and the dangers of a unipolar world. He also warned that some "people are trying to transform the OSCE into a vulgar instrument designed to promote the foreign policy interests of one or a group of countries."[5]

In the aftermath of the war in Georgia in 2008 there had been efforts to improve security and co-operation, including the "Corfu Process," designed to rebuild trust between states and take forward dialogue on Euro-Atlantic and Eurasian security.[6] There was also the "Towards a Security Community" declaration at the OSCE Summit in Astana in December 2010, which outlined the "vision of a free, democratic, common and indivisible Euro-Atlantic and Eurasian security community."[7] Unfortunately, the plan of action that was supposed to set benchmarks to achieve this vision was not adopted due to a lack of consensus and disagreements over ongoing conflicts in the OSCE area.

To provide some sense of direction, a decision was taken under Ireland's Chairpersonship in 2012 to take "a coordinated strategic approach" to reach the vision of Astana through the so-called "Helsinki +40 process."[8] This turned into more of an internal process of reforming the OSCE than a way of improving relations between Russia and the West. The process was eventually derailed with the annexation of Crimea and fighting in Luhansk and Donetsk in 2014.

Under Germany's Chairpersonship of the OSCE in 2016, a decision was taken at the Hamburg Ministerial Council to launch a "structured dialogue on the current and future challenges and risks to security in the OSCE area to foster a greater understanding on these issues that could serve as a common solid basis for a way forward."[9] This led to the establishment of the Structured Dialogue. However, there was no strategy behind how this process should be conducted, its chair changed almost every year, and there was insufficient political will from key states. As a result, five years of deliberations produced few results.

The need for a more strategic approach

When Thomas Greminger became Secretary General in 2017, he perceived the need for a more strategic approach. Having been Switzerland's ambassador to the OSCE during that country's Chairpersonship in 2014, he was all too aware of the gridlock within official OSCE dialogue formats and the need for fresh thinking. He was also concerned about the lack of interest among countries in chairing the Organization. He therefore wanted to strengthen the Secretariat's capacity to think strategically and to support the Chair.[10] To that end he decided to create a strategic policy planning cell. This was in line with his mandate to support the Chair "in all activities aimed at fulfilling the goals of the OSCE by, *inter alia*, providing expert advisory, material, technical and other support which may include background information, analysis, draft decisions, draft statements, summary records and archival support."[11]

Because of budgetary constraints and sensing that the idea might not enjoy support among all participating States at the outset, the Secretary General launched the unit as an extra-budgetary project. After a recruitment process, experts were hired by secondment from the Russian Federation, the United States, Finland, and later Switzerland.[12]

The Unit—soon renamed the Strategic Policy Support Unit (SPSU)—provided support to Chairpersonships (incoming and in office), gave strategic advice to the Secretary General, helped to co-ordinate the preparation of the program outline for the budget, and worked with relevant sections in the Secretariat to devise more strategic approaches to the Organization's programmatic activities (such as in Central Asia) and with Mediterranean partners. Much of the advice provided by the SPSU was oral or informal. One of the Unit's main impacts was to stimulate more strategic thinking within the Secretariat and Chairpersonships. The Unit also helped promote informal spaces for dialogue, such as the "Perspectives 20-30" agenda (focusing on youth), Security Days, Talking Points (speakers series), and the Cooperative Security Initiative. Furthermore, it carried out research including the production of a report (unpublished) entitled *Leadership, Continuity and Creativity: Towards a More Attractive Chairmanship Model*, which was discussed by representatives of previous and incoming Chairpersonships, and an internal paper on China and the OSCE.

At a time when resources were tight and trust in international organizations was low, the Unit tried to work with

OSCE executive structures to focus on areas where the OSCE could make a difference, to accentuate its added value, and to increase impact. A recurrent question in planning meetings was: "What can states do together in the OSCE that they cannot do alone or somewhere else?" Another question was "how to do less and do it better," instead of the usual mantra of "doing more with less" (because of zero nominal growth).

From the outset, the Unit was viewed with skepticism by some sections of the Secretariat and some OSCE delegations. Concerns were expressed about how the Unit was established: Some participating States felt that the idea could have been explained better to them and should have been agreed to by consensus. Others questioned whether and why the Secretary General should have a role in developing strategy for the Organization. Some argued that this is the prerogative of participating States. Others felt that the OSCE does not need a strategy, especially when dealing with the daily realities of the crisis in Ukraine. But as Lawrence Freedman has pointed out, "strategy comes into play where there is actual or potential conflict, when interests collide and forms of resolution are required."[13] It is precisely in times of crisis that one needs a strategy.

Slovak Foreign Minister Miroslav Lajcak, as OSCE Chair in 2019, understood this need. He tried to promote dialogue among ambassadors in Vienna and invited OSCE foreign ministers for an informal meeting in the High Tatras. He sought to promote common ground, consensus, and co-operation. While ministers were constructive during the meeting, this spirit was not reflected in the Permanent Council, and it did not translate into decisions at the Ministerial meeting in Bratislava in December 2019. With apparent frustration, Lajcak concluded the Slovak Chairpersonship with the unusual move of issuing a statement blasting the lack of consensus and concluding that "for me the only way to harness the potential of the Organization [...] is through political engagement, and political vision."[14]

Thomas Greminger took a similar approach, calling for a "common unifying agenda." Critics attacked him for allegedly trying to seek common ground at the expense of common principles and whispered that he was too close to Moscow, not least since some Russian diplomats had previously used the expression "unifying agenda." It was not even possible to get participating States to agree on a multi-year (or even two-year) program outline that would have enabled a more strategic approach to matching political priorities with resources. As a result, the critics and cynics prevailed: the Organization was crippled by competing, divisive, and often petty, even personal, agendas rather than a common, unifying one.

With participating States unwilling or unable to take a longer-term perspective, the Secretary General—in consultation with the Troika—supported the launch of a Cooperative Security Initiative. This project—carried out in co-operation with the Friedrich Ebert Stiftung and GLOBSEC—brought together eighteen experts from the OSCE area to stimulate people to think about why and how states need to work together for security and to deal with modern threats and challenges. This resulted in a report entitled *Restoring European Security* as well as a number of online products designed to provoke fresh thinking on "principled cooperation."[15] As the experts warned, "it must not take a major war to restore or build a new European security system."[16] The hope was that this Track II initiative could help set an agenda for co-operation that participating States would take up. This didn't happen, particularly because of the COVID-19 pandemic but also because there was no appetite among participating States to look for ways to de-escalate tensions or identify possible areas of co-operation for the future.

A strategy: Everybody's got one

There seems to be an aversion among the OSCE community to thinking strategically. Yet almost every national administration, company, and regional or international organization has a strategic policy or policy planning unit. It is standard practice. Almost every intergovernmental organization produces strategies. The EU has a number of strategic plans and launched a Strategic Compass early in 2022. NATO issued a new strategic concept in 2022 at the Madrid Summit "to equip the Alliance for security challenges and guide its future political and military development."[17] Regional organizations in other parts of the world are capable of long-term thinking; the African Union has its Agenda 2063, which is a 50-year plan adopted in 2013. The United Nations—which has three times more members than the OSCE—is able to come up with strategies and common goals. Why not the OSCE?

Perhaps it is a lack of imagination. Or, until recently, there may have been insufficient urgency. Maybe the lack of strategy is a good thing: Why waste time on negotiating or drafting nice words which have little impact? Defenders of this view would say that it is better to build peace on the ground than castles in the sky. Anyway, achieving consensus on a strategy on European security is almost impossible with so many states that are not like-minded and which no longer seem to share common assumptions or objectives. Furthermore, one must distinguish between the OSCE as a collection of states and OSCE executive structures. Although the OSCE has developed from being a conference to having executive structures, it is still led by its participating States. Indeed, the debate over the SPSU and the Secretary General's strategy-making role showed the unwillingness of some key countries to cede control over policy-relevant issues. And yet, it is clearly difficult to find common ground among fifty-seven national security strategies, especially if some countries regard each other as their biggest threat.

Whatever the reasons, the result is that the OSCE is constantly focused on its internal business, procedural issues, and the budget. There is seldom space to talk about bigger issues, despite the fact that there are so many of them. It is difficult to translate overall priorities into policy because no one can decide what the strategic priorities are. As a result, the

OSCE is trapped in a cycle of "business as usual" at precisely the moment when creative thinking and new approaches are urgently in demand. As Freedman has pointed out, "having a strategy suggests an ability to look up from the short term and the trivial to view the long term and the essential, to address causes rather than symptoms, to see woods rather than trees."[18] At the moment, the OSCE seems lost in the trees.

Recommendations: An iterative co-operative security agenda

Because of the war in Ukraine, it will be difficult for participating States to reach consensus on decisions in the Permanent or Ministerial Councils. It is hard to imagine an OSCE Summit with President Putin in attendance. Therefore, the OSCE's short-term strategy will be survival. However, muddling through and waiting for better days is not a way to plan for or shape the future. Hope is not a strategy. It is high time to start planning for a postwar Europe, and the OSCE is a logical place to do this. It should be an agent of change, not a product of it. But under the current circumstances, how can this be done?

The very act of working on a roadmap for stabilizing the situation in the OSCE area could provide a unifying agenda for OSCE participating States and give the Organization a sense of direction and purpose for the future. While the conditions are not the same as in 1972—since there is no consensus on the need for détente—the example of the Helsinki process from 1972 to 1975 is a good inspiration for how participating States could work together on rebuilding security and co-operation in Europe as a result of an iterative consultation process.

There is no need to have a consensus-based decision to launch such a process. It could be developed using existing structures and processes. Indeed, the fact that most meetings are taking place in informal settings at the moment lends itself well to open-ended dialogue on the building blocks of a more co-operative European security order.

Nevertheless, the process requires leadership. Therefore, the OSCE Troika could come up with a roadmap for benchmarks between now and a possible high-level meeting in 2025 to correspond with the fiftieth anniversary of the Helsinki Final Act. Thinking strategically, the Troika could briefly analyze the current challenges and security context and set out the desired ends of a co-operative security agenda. This would set a common agenda for the next three years and take pressure off consecutive Chairpersonships to come up with their own annual priorities.

A key focus of the co-operative security agenda will have to be politico-military aspects of security, namely arms control, including de-escalation, disarmament, and confidence- and security-building measures. Making peace in Ukraine will be difficult. Even after the fighting stops between Russia and Ukraine, it will be hard to rebuild trust, both between Ukraine and Russia and between Russia and the West. Nonetheless, the OSCE is well suited, well positioned, and well equipped to do this, building on the existing framework for arms control. It would make sense to agree on an agenda of the Forum for Security Co-operation and the Structured Dialogue to ensure that there is a common understanding of the issues to be discussed. This could be a sub-strategy of the overall co-operative security agenda.

Furthermore, the Vienna Document on confidence- and security-building measures should be modernized, for example to adjust the thresholds for notifications and inspections of military exercises, to limit the deployment of forces and equipment close to borders, and to reduce the risk of snap exercises. De-confliction measures could also be agreed to prevent incidents and accidents at sea and in the air. Opportunities should be created for military-to-military contacts, for example to discuss military doctrines, force postures, threat perceptions, and the impact of new technologies and weapons systems.

As in the 1980s, the OSCE could be the place to negotiate arms control agreements. Furthermore, it could be a forum to discuss security guarantees, for example for countries "in between" Russia and the West (especially those where Russian troops are still stationed), as well as for Russia in relation to NATO.

A co-operative security agenda could also reflect on how to interpret fundamental principles for peace and security in Europe in the current security environment. As the current OSCE Chairperson-in-Office Foreign Minister Rau of Poland has suggested, OSCE participating States should discuss how they understand these principles today and how OSCE principles and commitments can be implemented more effectively.[19]

Other issues that could be considered as part of the European security dialogue could include a legally binding Charter for the OSCE, reviewing the system of annual rotating Chairpersonships, strengthening mechanisms for the pacific settlement of disputes, reforming the human dimension implementation review process, looking at the impact of technology on human rights and the media, and revising the rules of procedure to prevent gridlock caused by a lack of consensus. Participating States should also identify issues that require co-operation but which were not anticipated in the OSCE's founding documents, such as transnational organized crime, terrorism, and the impact of climate change on security, cyber security, and migration. At a minimum, the strategy should be to preserve as much as possible of the OSCE's normative framework.

Unfortunately, the SPSU has been scaled down, and nothing similar has been created in its place. The Troika is focused on daily business and keeping the OSCE afloat, most participating States are reluctant to discuss a more co-operative future, and Russia continues to attack Ukraine. So where will a strategy come from?

In the short term, it may be prudent to discuss ideas informally in Track 1.5 processes involving external experts and a self-selecting group of countries that are "friends of the OSCE." This would give participating States (and the Troika) some degree of deniability to discuss ideas that may not enjoy consensus and without all fifty-seven participating States in attendance. But at the end of the day, decisions will have to be taken by participating States. Therefore, participating States—supported by the Secretariat—should at least use informal platforms for dialogue to think about and plan for the future.

Any strategy will obviously depend on the outcome of the war. Even those who think it is too early to discuss the future of European security must admit that it would be useful to have some ideas in the drawer for when it is time to start drawing up blueprints for the new security architecture. It is worth recalling that planning for a new international organization—which would eventually become the United Nations—started during the dark days of the Second World War, already in 1943.[20]

In short, now is the time for strategic thinking. The CSCE was designed to foster security and co-operation; during the Cold War it was not necessary to have co-operation in order to start discussing how to improve security. The OSCE cannot wait for stability to return to Europe—it should work towards it. Without a strategy, the OSCE has ended up in a place that is far from being the security community envisioned at the Astana Summit. It is time for a plan.

Notes

1 Walter Kemp also teaches at the Diplomatic Academy in Vienna and has recently published *Security and Cooperation: To the Same End* (Routledge, 2022). From 2018 to 2020 he was head of the Strategic Policy Support Unit in the office of the OSCE Secretary General.

2 Steven Heffington, Adam Oler, and David Tretler, eds., A National Security Strategy Primer (Washington, DC: National Defense University Press, 2019), p. 1, https://nwc.ndu.edu/Portals/71/Documents/Publications/NWC-Primer-FINAL_for%20Web.pdf?ver=HOH30gam-KOdUOM2RFoHRA%3D%3D

3 CSCE, Final Act (Helsinki: August 1, 1975), https://www.osce.org/files/f/documents/5/c/39501.pdf

4 CSCE, Charter of Paris for a New Europe (Paris: November 19–21, 1990), p. 12, https://www.osce.org/files/f/documents/0/6/39516.pdf

5 Vladimir Putin, Speech and the Following Discussion at the Munich Conference on Security Policy (Munich: February 10, 2007), http://en.kremlin.ru/events/president/transcripts/24034

6 OSCE, "Restoring Trust: The Corfu Process," December 1, 2010, https://www.osce.org/mc/87193

7 OSCE, Astana Commemorative Declaration, SUM.DOC/1/10/Corr.1* (Astana: December 3, 2010), p. 1, https://www.osce.org/files/f/documents/b/6/74985.pdf

8 OSCE, The OSCE Helsinki+40 Process, MC.DEC/3/12 (Dublin: December 7, 2012), p. 1, https://www.osce.org/files/f/documents/e/0/98309.pdf

9 OSCE, From Lisbon to Hamburg: Declaration on the Twentieth Anniversary of the OSCE Framework for Arms Control, MC.DOC/4/16 (Hamburg: December 9, 2016), p. 1, https://www.osce.org/files/f/documents/3/e/289496.pdf

10 Thomas Greminger, "Strengthening Co-operative Security in Difficult Times: Three Years as Secretary General of the OSCE (2017–2020) – a Critical Appraisal," in *Multilateralism in Transition: Challenges and Opportunities for the OSCE,*

eds. Simon J. A. Mason and Lisa Watanabe (Zürich: Center for Security Studies [CSS], ETH Zürich, 2021), 22–84; Thomas Greminger, Making the OSCE More Effective: Practical Recommendations from a Former Secretary General, IFSH (ed.), OSCE Insights 1/2021 (Baden-Baden: Nomos, 2022), https://doi.org/10.5771/9783748911456-01

11 OSCE, Role of the OSCE Secretary General, MC.DEC/15/04 (Sofia: December 7, 2004), p. 1, https://www.osce.org/files/f/documents/2/0/29705.pdf

12 The Unit was headed by the author, Walter Kemp (Canadian).

13 Lawrence Freedman, *Strategy: A History* (Oxford: Oxford University Press, 2013), xi.

14 Miroslav Lajcak, OSCE Chairperson-in-Office and Minister for Foreign and European Affairs of Slovakia (Bratislava: December 20, 2019), https://www.osce.org/chairmanship/442771

15 Walter Kemp and Reinhard Krumm, eds., *Restoring European Security: From Managing Relations to Principled Cooperation* (Vienna: Friedrich Ebert Stiftung, 2021).

16 Kemp and Krumm, cited above (Note 15), p. 39.

17 NATO, "Strategic Concepts," November 29, 2021, https://www.nato.int/cps/en/natohq/topics_56626.htm

18 Freedman, cited above (Note 13), p. ix.

19 Website of the Republic of Poland, "Minister Zbigniew Rau Inaugurates Renewed OSCE European Security Dialogue in Vienna," February 8, 2022, https://www.gov.pl/web/osce/minister-zbigniew-rau-inaugurates-renewed-osce-european-security-dialogue-in-vienna

20 Stephen C. Schlesinger, *Act of Creation: The Founding of the United Nations* (Cambridge, MA: Westview Press, 2003).

The OSCE in Crisis: Five Lessons from the League of Nations

Mette Eilstrup-Sangiovanni[*]

Abstract

Since the Russian invasion of Ukraine in February 2022, questions about the survival of the OSCE have taken an acute form. However, the war in Ukraine is not the only crisis facing the OSCE. The Organization has long been challenged by institutional deadlock, boycotts, budget cuts, increasing great power conflict, and growing contestation from nationalist and populist leaders. The question is therefore: How can the OSCE respond to such challenges to increase its resilience? In this paper I analyze various historical crises faced by the League of Nations and consider the extent to which institutional "coping strategies" during this era offer lessons for the present. Although the League was ultimately dissolved, many of its individual agencies live on in the United Nations. The paper provides recommendations for how to apply lessons from the League with a view to strengthening the OSCE's resilience.

Keywords

OSCE, Ukraine conflict, organizational survival, interwar period, League of Nations

To cite this publication: Mette Eilstrup-Sangiovanni, "The OSCE in Crisis: Five Lessons from the League of Nations," in *OSCE Insights*, eds. Cornelius Friesendorf and Argyro Kartsonaki (Baden-Baden: Nomos, 2023), https://doi.org/10.5771/9783748933625-03

Introduction

Since the early 2000s, OSCE supporters have wrestled with how the Organization can contribute to resolving conflicts in the territories of the former Soviet Union and de-escalate growing tensions between Russia and the West. Lately, this question has taken an acute form: How can the OSCE survive large-scale warfare between two of its participating States? How can the Organization survive growing hostility from participating States so that it may contribute to future European security dialogue and confidence-building?

The literature in International Relations has considered how joint membership in international organizations (IOs) can reduce the risk of inter-state war, but less attention has been paid to how IOs can survive violent conflicts among member states. Viewed from a historical perspective, the OSCE's survival odds look slim. Looking at the survivability of IOs across the past two centuries, studies have found that security organizations have

* Mette Eilstrup-Sangiovanni
University of Cambridge
mer29@cam.ac.uk

the lowest survival rates, with organizational deaths peaking during times of war or economic crisis.[1] The Great Depression and the world wars killed off most existing security-focused IOs.[2] History also offers examples of IOs terminating due to violent conflict among pairs of member states. The Development Bank of the Great Lakes States was terminated after Rwanda invaded Zaire[3] in 1996 to defeat rebel groups taking refuge there in the wake of the 1994 Rwandan civil war. Italy's invasion of Ethiopia in 1935 is widely said to have undermined the League of Nations (LoN), although previous failures to check inter-state aggression had already shaken its foundations. If these historical examples are anything to go by, the outlook for the OSCE is bleak.

The war in Ukraine is far from the only crisis facing the OSCE: institutional deadlock, boycotts, budget cuts, increasing great power conflict, and growing contestation from nationalist and populist leaders all present acute challenges to the OSCE. How can the OSCE respond to such challenges to increase its resilience? In considering this question, it is instructive to explore how economic crises, great power conflicts, and nationalist populism have affected IOs in the past. The last period of hyper-nationalism, de-globalization, and democratic backsliding began in the late 1920s and lasted until the end of World War II. Protectionism rose, authoritarian populism spread in Europe and beyond, and both great powers and smaller states turned away from the LoN and other multilateral organizations towards ad hoc, bilateral diplomacy.[4] Many IOs were terminated during this period or saw their memberships and mandates reduced. Others, however —including many League agencies—survived and continued to expand their functions.

This paper looks "under the hood" of the LoN and other IOs during the interwar period and examines whether the "coping strategies" they employed hold lessons for the OSCE. My analysis draws on recently released archival records of the League and previous academic research. International organization archives contain official documents (conference proceedings, speeches, working papers, official reports, treaties, agreements) and operational information such as internal briefing papers, budgets, staffing reports, and the correspondence of senior staff. These sources provide crucial insights regarding the goals, interests, and perceived challenges faced by IOs during geopolitical crises, allowing us to drill further into the important detail of how IO agents perceive and manage member state conflict and pushback against their authority.

Looking to the LoN for lessons about IO resilience may seem unorthodox. The League has long been regarded as a failed experiment in international co-operation. Recently, however, international historians and IR scholars have begun to reassess the League's legacy, pointing out that important elements of its institutional structures have lived on in the UN.[5] In rewriting the League's legacy, scholars have considered the ways in which its Secretariat and staff shaped its evolution during its twenty-five-year existence, providing detailed evidence of how its central institutions—in co-operation with supportive member states and transnational actors—wrestled with membership strife, treaty denunciations, shrinking budgets, and populist push-back (with varying degrees of success). Although the League was ultimately dissolved, these individual fights for survival can teach us much about how IOs battle adversity. Ultimately, we can learn from failure as well as success. In what follows, I consider various dimensions of crisis faced by the League and other interwar IOs and conclude with recommendations for how lessons can be applied to the OSCE today.

Budget crisis

A major challenge facing the OSCE is a steady reduction in its annual budget (in real terms).[6] In this regard, the OSCE has much in common with the League. The League began its activities in 1920 at a time of considerable economic distress and national opposition to "wasteful" international institutions given the destitution caused by war. Between 1922 and 1926, the League's budget increased by only 5 percent, while its employed staff grew by 27 percent.[7] To economize on resources, traveling was discouraged; documents and minutes could not always be printed.[8]

Yet such penny-pinching fell far short of balancing the books, and therefore ways for the League to fulfill its tasks had to be found. Since the chief task of the Secretariat was to gather and disseminate information, issue recommendations, and produce expert reports, agreements were reached with individual governments and other IOs to gather and disseminate their research and statistical data, thus reducing operational costs.[9] Another way to cut costs was to lean on private actors. From 1922, the American Rockefeller Foundation made a series of grants to the League's Health Organization (LHO). During the 1930s, these amounted to approximately half a million Swiss francs per year.[10] Between 1933 and 1942, the Rockefeller Foundation also funded research by the Secretariat's Economic Intelligence Service on combatting economic depression, contributing one-third of its budget at its peak.[11] Likewise, the League's substantial investigations into trafficking in women and children were funded by the American Bureau of Social Hygiene.[12]

In addition to private foundations, labor and peace movements also played a significant role in supporting the League's institutions. During the 1920s and 1930s, women's peace activists, labor unions, and scholars gathered at transnational conferences to campaign against war and imperialism. National League of Nations societies and NGOs campaigned for the ratification of the League's Permanent Court and supported its technical, economic, social, and humanitarian work.[13] To facilitate such links, Secretariat officials frequently attended meetings of international NGOs and promoted NGO access not only to the Secretariat but also to the Council and the Assembly.[14]

Partnering with private actors served several purposes. First, amidst tight budgetary constraints, NGOs and civil society groups brought additional expertise, knowledge, and funds to the League. More broadly, it was hoped that involvement by civil society and NGOs would increase public support by bringing the League closer to the public. Civil society actors were also relied on to scrutinize state claims and politics towards the League, thus preempting national political mobilization based on scapegoating the League and enabling citizens to better evaluate political claims. For example, the League appointed NGO "assessors" to its committees on communications and transit, social policy, teaching, trafficking in women, and refugees.[15] Finally, by allying with subnational and transnational actors, League institutions sought to broaden their bases of political and material support beyond governments to political agents within and across member states.

These examples may offer lessons for the OSCE. During the past decade, the OSCE's operational capacity has steadily declined due to a decrease in seconded personnel and financial support. Expecting participating States to increase their financial contributions in the current climate would be wishful thinking. Instead, the OSCE might adopt the League's strategy of building strategic partnerships with subnational, transnational, and supranational actors—including municipal governments, NGOs, private foundations and businesses, and IOs—that have complementary epistemic and material resources, using these to fill gaps in operational capacities.[16] Allying with substate and transnational actors simultaneously increased the resources available to the League and helped to improve its perceived legitimacy through epistemic validation, by serving to discredit state criticism and by influencing state policy "from within." Transnational alliances also served in some cases to lessen tight state control by supplementing or replacing government funds with private funds and expertise.

Hiding from harm: Great power conflict and institutional retrenchment

Operating in an environment of growing nationalism and great power conflict, the League had a difficult start, especially in facilitating co-operation on issues seen to entail high sovereignty costs. A Convention for the Control of the Trade in Arms and Ammunition was signed in September 1919 but never came into force as France declined to ratify it.[17] A Draft Treaty of Mutual Assistance, which outlawed wars of aggression, was rejected by governments in 1924. The Geneva Protocol of 1924, which created a system of compulsory arbitration, likewise faltered as Britain refused to sign.[18]

Given repeated failures of disarmament co-operation and amid growing political tension, the League's Disarmament Section and the Secretariat adopted a new strategy of "hide and retrench." Between 1930 and 1934, the Secretariat carefully avoided bringing proposals it deemed doomed to fail before the Council. Meetings of the General Commission and the Disarmament Section were repeatedly canceled or postponed as leading bureaucrats considered it better not to convene the League's disarmament committees than to allow meetings to become a stage for public displays of animosity and megaphone diplomacy.[19] As Sir Drummond reflected after Italy's invasion of Ethiopia in 1935: "If the League emerges successfully from the Ethiopia-Italo ordeal the prospects will be bright for a convention to adjust armaments. If not, the whole position will have to be revised [...]. In any event, until next year, the less said about disarmament the better."[20]

The moratorium on high-level conferences did not, however, imply the end of active disarmament diplomacy. Rather than convening full intergovernmental conferences, the Secretariat turned its efforts to organizing meetings among smaller groups of like-minded states with the aim of building consensus around limited, practical objectives. It also began collecting and analyzing data on national armaments. Making this data widely available, it was hoped, would help to generate public pressure on governments and might serve as a starting point for future arms control negotiations. That hope was never realized, but had governments been willing to discuss disarmament, the League would have had extensive data on hand as a basis for negotiations.

Trade co-operation underwent a similar development. As economic nationalism intensified following the Wall Street crash of 1929, a series of intergovernmental trade conferences failed.[21] Unable to influence political aspects of trade such as tariffs and customs, the League's economic institutions abandoned plans for further trade conferences. Instead, efforts by senior officials in the Secretariat focused on improving the League's machinery for economic diplomacy. Henceforth, the Economic Committee focused on resolving legal and administrative problems that acted as indirect barriers to trade—for example commercial arbitration, the simplification of customs formalities, and the standardization of statistical methods and customs terminology.[22] Another area for expansion was research and publication of economic data. In 1931, the Secretariat published a report entitled *The Course and Phases of the World-Economic Depression*. Addressing the danger that states might object to any findings that were politically sensitive, Alexander Loveday, Director of the Economic, Financial, and Transit Section, recommended that the analytical side of the research "be subordinated to its fact finding aspects [...] since, ultimately, the findings would speak for themselves."[23] In short, to avoid alienating states, the Economic Section stuck to producing "neutral" research, leaving outside experts to draw unpopular conclusions.

"Hide and retrench" presented an obvious strategy for League institutions dealing with the politically sensitive issues of armaments and trade, yet less overtly political IOs navigated nationalist backlash in similar ways. From its birth in 1929 until the war, the International Bureau of Education (IBE) was highly active despite a limited budget and staff.[24] Launched in 1934, the IBE's "pedagogical tour of the world," which collected data on national educational reforms and issued recommendations, reached more than seventy countries and provided a crucial resource for national education reformers. During World War II, the IBE's Secretariat collaborated with the International Red Cross to create the Service of Intellectual Assistance to Prisoners of War, which provided prisoners of war with books. Thanks to the broad appeal of such activities, the IBE's membership grew from twelve in 1929 to twenty by the end of the war, spanning Europe and Latin America. Undoubtedly, a crucial factor in the IBE's resilience was its apolitical, technical nature, which insulated it from political strife. This apolitical nature reflected a deliberate choice. Many governments were suspicious of international meddling in their domestic affairs and of a perceived Western bias in the global education agenda. To avoid political controversy, the IBE "ceaselessly stayed clear of interfering with [the] educational freedom of partners."[25] Rather than pushing for the standardization of national approaches, the Bureau strove to promote universal education without interfering with "local priorities," leaving specific recommendations and implementation to local authorities and NGOs. The IBE survives to this day as a specialized agency of UNESCO (IBE-UNESCO).

What are the possible lessons for the OSCE in this context? During the last few decades, arms control and disarmament—centerpieces of the OSCE's agenda—have become increasingly difficult as both the United States and Russia have pulled out of major arms control treaties.[26] Hence, many argue in favor of seeking to revive disarmament discussions and strengthening the OSCE's role in arms control verification.[27] Yet any present attempt to update the 2011 Vienna Document on confidence- and security-building or to relaunch conventional arms control within the scope of the Structured Dialogue (initiated by the German Chairperson-in-Office in 2016) or the group of like-minded countries in the Berlin format would likely be fruitless.[28]

The same is true for human rights initiatives. As the relationship between Russia and the West has deteriorated, debates on human rights have descended into ideological confrontation, leading to institutional blockages.[29] It seems counterproductive to table new initiatives or to seek to rekindle existing ones against such opposition. The Helsinki and Paris Charters would not be agreed by OSCE states today any more than the League's Covenant would have been agreed in 1935. It is therefore futile to insist on their enforcement in the current climate. As long as agreement remains elusive, individual states should seek to build greater confidence and trust by engaging in specific projects within the OSCE to increase transparency, or by using coalitions of the willing to advance specific projects. Such minilateral measures may not achieve much in the short term but would be more productive in the current climate than attempting to push ambitious schemes on which no agreement can be found.

Exploiting a flexible mandate

By 1934, the League's intergovernmental activities had mostly ceased. Had its mandate been limited to conventional security co-operation and trade, its operations would have ended. However, a broad mandate based on a comprehensive approach to security allowed the League's institutions to explore new areas of activity, including transportation, literacy, nutrition, and sanitation. An important focus for the League's social and economic institutions during the latter half of the 1930s was to outline a common front against poverty and disease as root causes of conflict.[30] This task was deemed to be of greater potential appeal to states and wider publics than the controversial issues of trade and disarmament.

Co-operation on social matters and broad conflict prevention tasks also allowed the League to gain supporters beyond its core member states. Two conferences were held in Java in 1937—one on combating trafficking in women, another on rural hygiene. In June 1936, the League's Health Organization held a session in Moscow, the only League institution to ever meet there.[31] Links between Soviet health authorities and the LHO offered an ideal opportunity to forge practical connections in an apolitical domain. Ravaged by civil war, famine, and disease, Soviet health institutions were under severe strain. Hence, despite widespread fear and mistrust between Russia and Western governments, a special commission was founded to investigate typhus in Russia.[32] By 1935, collaboration on communicable diseases and intellectual matters had helped pave the way for Russia's inclusion as a formal member of the League.[33]

In sum, as geopolitical conflict in Europe intensified, there was a change in the work of the League's institutions. Rather than attempting to gain agreement on divisive issues of trade and military security, they focused on issues where common ground could be found.[34] At the same time, they exploited a broad mandate to tailor activities to the needs of countries outside Europe, thereby broadening political support and patronage.[35] This strategy proved particularly successful for the LHO. Despite the financial restrictions imposed by the General Assembly, the generosity of private supporters allowed the LHO to continuously expand its activities. Early on, its focus broadened from epidemiological work in Eastern Europe to addressing health problems in Asia and Africa. NGOs, leading scientific institutes, and individual experts from all over the world freely contributed their knowledge and time to it, increasing its autonomy from states and helping it to transcend great power conflict.[36] In 1945, rather than being dissolved, the LHO was transformed into the World Health Organization.

While clearly a different kind of institution than the LHO, the OSCE can nevertheless take inspiration from this success story. Entrusted with a broad array of activities—from combatting human trafficking, radicalization, and terrorism to promoting economic connectivity and building scientific expertise on climate issues—the OSCE is well placed to reduce threats to its existence by widening its activities and thereby its appeal to diverse states. While state funding is likely to be scarce for the foreseeable future, partnering with non-state actors may help to increase the financial and technical resources available to the OSCE, increasing autonomy from governments in the process. For their part, many NGOs are likely to welcome the political access and added legitimacy that may come from collaboration with an intergovernmental organization.

Harnessing institutional complexity

A major challenge confronting the OSCE which the League did not face to the same extent is competition from other IOs. Despite strengthening the OSCE with the 1990 Paris Charter, Western states have prioritized co-operation within NATO and the EU, while Russia has supported the creation of alternative regional organizations which address various aspects of collective security and economic and political stability, including the Commonwealth of Independent States (CIS), the Collective Security Treaty Organization (CSTO), the Shanghai Cooperation Organisation (SCO), and the Eurasian Economic Union (EAEU). In conjunction with the overlapping mandates and activities of UN agencies like the UN Development Programme (UNDP), the UN Economic Commission for Europe (UNECE), and the UN Office on Drugs and Crime (UNODC), this has led to a proliferation of overlapping and potentially competing institutions in the OSCE space. Historically, institutional overlap has sometimes contributed to organizational deaths, as competition for scarce resources has put some IOs out of business.[37] However, institutional overlap can also be turned into a strength, provided IOs achieve a level of specialization and division of labor that prevents states from "forum shopping" or playing organizations off against one another.[38] In this case, co-ordination and collaboration between IOs can help to increase value for money for states while giving potentially competing IOs a positive stake in one another's flourishing.

In recent years, the EU has been a major funder of the OSCE in areas where institutional interests converge. The two organizations have many interests in common, including good governance and fighting organized crime and corruption. Yet given Russian animosity towards the EU, the OSCE must not be perceived simply as an instrument of EU security interests; it must clearly articulate its own agenda.[39] In addition to collaborating with the EU, the OSCE would gain from deepening co-operation with relevant UN agencies, such as UNODC, UNDP, and the UN High Commissioner for Refugees.[40] Co-operation with regional organizations such as the CIS, the CSTO, and the EAEU will also be important. Some might worry that the different values embodied in these organizations present a barrier to co-operation; as former Secretary General Thomas Greminger points out, however, for reasons of politico-geographical balance, it is crucial to engage organizations both east and west of Vienna. For example, with the SCO, common ground may be found in the fight against violent extremism and terrorism in Central Asia.[41]

International organizations can survive and thrive in a crowded institutional space either by developing niche functions and tools that render their services unique compared to those of other IOs or by playing a co-ordinating role, acting as convenors and building bridges between other IOs—or between international and national organizations. The OSCE is well placed to do both. For example, combatting violent extremism is one domain in which the OSCE has its own distinctive tools compared to other IOs. Given its extensive field experience, the OSCE is often better placed than NATO or the EU to reach out to local NGOs and municipal authorities. Compared to these organizations, the OSCE is also more likely to be accepted as a neutral mediator or monitor on the ground. Finally, the OSCE "focuses on promoting a comprehensive approach to cyber security, particularly in Central Asia, where NATO and the EU have a limited presence."[42] In terms of convening power, the OSCE's broad membership, which intersects with the membership of NATO, the EU, the SCO, and the CSTO, puts it in a good position to play the role of convenor and inter-institutional co-ordinator.

Conclusions and recommendations

Significant care must be taken in applying lessons from the 1930s to the present or in comparing a "multi-purpose" IO like the League of Nations to the OSCE. Still, the two organizations have strong similarities, above all their comprehensive approach to co-operative security and a membership which spans deep political and ideological divides. What's more, present challenges to the OSCE carry strong echoes of the period leading to the downfall of the League. Much like the League during the 1920s and 1930s, the OSCE is operating in a climate of economic instability and austerity. Both organizations have seen political conflict trigger direct challenges to their founding principles. Just as Italy, Japan, and Germany violated the collective security clause of the League's Charter, we have seen a series of grave violations of the OSCE's founding documents, starting with NATO's bombardment of the Federal Republic of Yugoslavia in 1999 and continuing with Putin's war in Chechnya that same year, Russia's war in Georgia in 2008, the annexation of Crimea in 2014, and military aggression against Ukraine in 2014 and 2022.

Given the magnitude of these challenges, it is clear that the OSCE needs a recipe for surviving both the immediate crisis triggered by the Ukraine war and the wider onslaught against its authority and the hollowing out of its resources. What can be done? Looking back at events during the 1930s, many have blamed the League for not doing enough to uphold the Charter's collective security provisions, which called for automatic sanctions and armed defense of the territorial status quo.[43] Likewise, some have called for harsher diplomatic sanctions against Russia, and Ukraine has demanded its expulsion from the OSCE.[44]

This is a high-risk strategy with uncertain benefits, however. When threatened with economic and military sanctions by other member states, Germany swiftly withdrew from the League and announced its full rearmament. If pushed too far into a corner, Russia may simply leave the OSCE, perhaps taking others with it. Although this would not necessarily spell the end of the OSCE, it would rob it of a major part of its *raison d'être*.

To overcome present woes, others have called for institutional reform to strengthen the autonomy of the OSCE's Secretary General and to extend the one-year budget cycle to prevent quarreling governments from taking the budget "hostage."[45] While such reforms would be positive for the OSCE in the long run, they would achieve little in the short term, since they would fail to address the political nature of the current crisis. As Byron Hunt observed in his study of the Italo-Ethiopian war, IOs "rely as much on a common will to maintain themselves as they do on their constituted authority. If the League failed where the United Nations has not, it was because of the lack of this will in the former, and not because the latter is a better constituted organization."[46] In the same way, the OSCE's present crisis is not primarily "constitutional" but unmistakably political. Institutional reform will not fix that.

If neither the expulsion of non-compliant states nor institutional reform presents a viable strategy for survival, what can participating States do to enhance the OSCE's resilience? My analysis suggests five specific strategies for harnessing the OSCE's institutional strengths.

Retrench and diversify. A consensus-based organization like the OSCE (or the League) cannot be (much) more than the sum of the will of its participating States. Therefore, the OSCE's greatest asset may be its broad mandate, which provides flexibility to focus on tasks where *some* agreement can be found. The OSCE should exploit its flexible mandate to take a tempered approach—for now—to highly divisive issues like human rights and disarmament and should instead focus on less contentious issues like combatting radicalization, terrorism, human trafficking, and organized crime, as well as promoting co-operation on "low political issues" like economic connectivity, water diplomacy, and the security implications of climate change in order to reduce tensions. Producing consensual (and fact-based) knowledge about such problems should be highlighted as a key institutional deliverable. This does not mean abandoning the OSCE's core mandate but rather limiting its activities in these domains to promoting informal dialogue and building consensus among smaller groups who may contribute extra-budgetary funds to undertake specific programmatic initiatives. Clearly, such activities must be carefully designed to avoid alienating non-participants. Field activities outside Europe, in Central Asia, or focused on relatively non-contentious issues like transnational crime may be particularly fruitful targets.

Broaden political support. History teaches us that IOs thrive by cultivating a broad base of political support. A clear asset in this respect is the OSCE's large and heterogeneous membership. While it may often lead to deadlock and lowest-common-denominator agreements, a large and heterogeneous membership means that an IO may lose active support or interest from some states while still retaining relevance to others that continue to see it as worthwhile. Indeed, having a large and heterogeneous membership has historically been a strong predictor of IO survivability.[47] The OSCE should therefore focus on engaging the *whole* of its membership, for example by pivoting towards a stronger focus on security-building in Central Asia.

Broaden bases of patronage. Most IOs lean on different sponsors during their lifespan. As the OSCE's budget continues to decline in real terms, it should strive to build stronger alliances with NGOs and subnational and supranational actors that share its objectives and that have complementary financial and technical resources that can be used to fill critical gaps in institutional and operational capacities.

Plan ahead. The OSCE does not have the political or technical capacity to engage in military crisis resolution. For now, it must therefore seek to "ride out the storm" by retreating from politically sensitive areas such as human rights promotion, arms control, and the policing of unstable ceasefires to focus on providing other benefits to supportive states. This does not mean taking its eyes off the Ukraine conflict. Rather, OSCE officials—in collaboration with like-minded states—should be ready with a plan of engagement if and when a ceasefire is agreed. This is especially important given that the OSCE is surrounded by institutional "competitors"—for example the EU, the UN, and NATO—with bigger budgets who will also be ready to get involved. Here, the OSCE must prepare to use its unique convening power as the largest co-operative security organization in the world to co-ordinate the efforts of other IOs.

Plan B. Finally, the OSCE leadership should focus on articulating a Plan B should the present conflict fail to be resolved. A key lesson from history is that organizational flexibility is essential to survival. OSCE supporters should ask: If Russia were to disengage, where would that leave the OSCE? Does it have sufficient institutional assets to maintain its appeal to its remaining participants and thus give it a continued *raison d'être*? In such a scenario, offering a durable platform for dialogue between European and (some) Eurasian states and leaving the door open for Russia's eventual return might be one of the strongest arguments for keeping the OSCE alive.

Notes

1 Mette Eilstrup-Sangiovanni, "Death of International Organizations: The Organizational Ecology of Intergovernmental Organizations, 1815–2015," *Review of International Organizations* 15, no. 2 (2020): 339–70; Mette Eilstrup-Sangiovanni, "What Kills International Organisations? When and Why International Organisations Terminate," *European Journal of International Relations* 27, no. 1 (2021): 281–310.

2 For example the Suez Canal Administration (dissolved 1914), the Reparations Commission (dissolved 1933), the Inter-Allied Rhineland High Commission

(dissolved 1934), the European Commissions for Control of the Oder and Elbe (dissolved 1936), the European Commission of the Danube (dissolved 1939), the Committee on Non-Intervention in Spanish Affairs (dissolved 1939), the Committee of Imperial Defence (dissolved 1940), and the League of Nations (dissolved 1946).

3 The present-day Democratic Republic of Congo.

4 League of Nations, Economic Intelligence Service, *The Network of World Trade: A Companion Volume to "Europe's Trade"* (Geneva: League of Nations, 1942), 1:90–91.

5 M. Patrick Cottrell, *The League of Nations: Enduring Legacies of the First Experiment at World Organization* (New York: Routledge, 2018); Susan Pedersen, "Back to the League of Nations," *American Historical Review* 112, no. 4 (2007): 1091–1117.

6 United States Mission to the OSCE, Statement on the Presentation of the 2022 Unified Budget Proposal by the Secretary General, PC.DEL/1590/21 (Vienna: October 21, 2021), https://www.osce.org/files/f/documents/8/4/502990.pdf

7 F. P. Walters, *A History of the League of Nations* (New York: Oxford University Press, 1952), 174. See also "General Report Adopted by the Assembly on September 27th, 1927," *League of Nations Official Journal* 9, no. 1 (January 1928): i–vii.

8 Walters, cited above (Note 7), pp. 133–34.

9 A. Alexander Menzies, "Technical Assistance and the League of Nations," in *The League of Nations in Retrospect: Proceedings of the Symposium Organized by the United Nations Library and the Graduate Institute of International Studies, Geneva, 6–9 November 1980* (Berlin: De Gruyter, 1983), 295–312. See also Cost, Printing and Distribution of Monthly Bulletin of Statistics, 1921, R309/10/12065/6408, United Nations Archives at Geneva.

10 Health Organisation – Rockefeller Foundation – Financial Cooperation 1937, 1937–1938, R6040/8A/27171/546, United Nations Archives at Geneva. This corresponds to some 9–10 million Swiss francs by present-day values.

11 "First Meeting (Private)," *League of Nations Official Journal* 19, no. 2 (February 1938): 74–77; Disarmament Conference – Progress Reports of the President of the Conference to the Bureau, 1933–1934, R4220/7B/10742/596, United Nations Archives at Geneva; Kathryn Lavelle, "Exit, Voice, and Loyalty in International Organizations: US Involvement in the League of Nations," *Review of International Organizations* 2, no. 4 (2007): 380.

12 Pedersen, cited above (Note 5).

13 Craig Murphy, *International Organization and Industrial Change: Global Governance since 1850* (Cambridge: Polity Press, 1994).

14 Thomas Richard Davies, "A 'Great Experiment' of the League of Nations Era: International Nongovernmental Organizations, Global Governance, and Democracy beyond the State," *Global Governance* 18, no. 4 (2012): 405–23; Steve Charnovitz, "Learning from Early NGO Activity," *Proceedings of the Annual Meeting (American Society of International Law)* 92 (April 1–4 1998): 338–41.

15 Davies, cited above (Note 14), p. 409; Alfred Zimmern, *The League of Nations and the Rule of Law, 1918–1935*, 2nd ed. (London: Macmillan, 1939).

16 David Galbreath, André Härtel, and Stefan Wolff, "Towards a More Strategic Partnership: Strengthening the OSCE through Enhanced EU-OSCE Cooperation," in *OSCE Insights*, ed. IFSH (Baden-Baden: Nomos, 2022), https://doi.org/10.5771/9783748911456-03; Ranjit Lall, "Beyond Institutional Design: Explaining

the Performance of International Organizations," *International Organization* 71, no. 2 (2017): 245–80.

17 Traffic in Arms, 7 May 1920, R186/8/4407/4407, United Nations Archives at Geneva.

18 Record of Th. Achnides's conversations in London during his mission to attend Mr Henderson's funeral. "Disarmament Conference – Correspondence between the Secretariat and the President of the Conference," R4220/7B/10257/596/ Jacket 4, United Nations Archives at Geneva.

19 Memoranda on Disarmament Forwarded by the Foreign Office London, 1934, R4220/7B/10829/596, United Nations Archives at Geneva; Pedersen, cited above (Note 5).

20 As reported by Th. Achnides, cited above (Note 18).

21 Martin D. Dubin, "Toward the Bruce Report: The Economic and Social Programs of the League of Nations in the Avenol Era," in *The League of Nations in Retrospect: Proceedings of the Symposium Organized by the United Nations Library and the Graduate Institute of International Studies, Geneva, 6–9 November 1980* (Berlin: De Gruyter, 1983), 42–72.

22 Alexander Loveday, "The Economic and Financial Activities of the League," *International Affairs* 17, no. 6 (1938): 788–808; Menzies, cited above (Note 9).

23 Lavelle, cited above (Note 11), p. 379.

24 Pedro Rosselló, *Conférence internationale de l'instruction publique, Recommandations 1934–1977* (Geneva: UNESCO-BIE, 1961).

25 Rita Hofstetter and Bernard Schneuwly, "The International Bureau of Education (1925–1968): A Platform for Designing a 'Chart of World Aspirations for Education,'" *European Educational Research Journal* 12, no. 2 (2013): 217.

26 For example, Russia withdrew from the Treaty on Conventional Armed Forces in Europe in 2015, and both the United States and Russia withdrew from the Open Skies Treaty in 2020 and 2021, respectively.

27 Benjamin Schaller, Strengthening the Role of the OSCE in Times of Increased Tensions and Emerging Crisis Situations: The Untapped Potential in the European Arms Control Framework (Geneva: Geneva Centre for Security Policy, 2021), https://dam.gcsp.ch/files/doc/strengthening-the-role-of-the-osce-in-times-of-increased-tensions-and-emerging-crisis-situations; Galbreath, Härtel, and Wolff, cited above (Note 16); Swiss Federal Department of Foreign Affairs, "The Presentation of the New OSCE Action Plan in Vienna Sends a Strong Signal," January 13, 2022, https://www.eda.admin.ch/eda/en/fdfa/fdfa/aktuell/newsuebersicht/2022/01/aktionsplan-osze-2025.html

28 Twenty-two states participate in the German-led group of like-minded countries on conventional arms control, but major players like the United States, Canada, Poland, and the Baltic states and Norway remain aloof.

29 Stefan Lehne, Reviving the OSCE: European Security and the Ukraine Crisis (Washington, DC: Carnegie Endowment for International Peace, 2015), https://www.jstor.org/stable/resrep12952#metadata_info_tab_contents; David Galbreath, "Putting the Colour into Revolutions? The OSCE and Civil Society in the Post-Soviet Region," *Journal of Communist Studies and Transition Politics* 25, nos. 2–3 (2009): 161–80.

30 Walters, cited above (Note 7), p. 575.

31 Ingeborg Plettenberg, "The Soviet Union and the League of Nations," in *The League of Nations in Retrospect: Proceedings of the Symposium Organized by the United Nations Library and the Graduate Institute of International Studies, Geneva,*

6–9 November 1980 (Berlin: De Gruyter, 1983), 156.

32 Epidemics in Russia, 29 August 1921, R824/12B/15319/15255, United Nations Archives at Geneva. See also Plettenberg, cited above (Note 31).

33 Plettenberg, cited above (Note 31), p. 156.

34 Walters, cited above (Note 7), p. 750.

35 Thomas Müller, "Institutional Reforms and the Politics of Inequality Reproduction: The Case of the League of Nations' Council Crisis in 1926," *Global Society* 34, no. 3 (2020): 304–17.

36 Health Organisation, 28 August 1919, R811-1/12B/921/126, United Nations Archives at Geneva; Plague Epidemic, 28 August 1925, R815/12B/6646/5568, United Nations Archives at Geneva; Establishment of Medical or Sanitary Section under the League of Nations, 4 July 1919, R811-1/12B/126/126, United Nations Archives at Geneva; Karen Gram-Skjoldager and Haakon Andreas Ikonomou, "The League of Nations Secretariat: An Experiment in Liberal Internationalism?," *Monde(s)* 19, no. 1 (2021): 31–50.

37 Eilstrup-Sangiovanni, "What Kills International Organizations?," cited above (Note 1); Mette Eilstrup-Sangiovanni and Oliver Westerwinter, "The Global Governance Complexity Cube: Varieties of Institutional Complexity in Global Governance," *Review of International Organizations* 17, no. 2 (2022): 233–62.

38 C. Randall Henning and Tyler Pratt, "Hierarchy and Differentiation in International Regime Complexes: A Theoretical Framework for Comparative Research" (unpublished paper, 2022), https://static1.squarespace.com/static/5c54747ad7819e06b909fb1f/t/61f351dd6cf4da0b9d3d2eed/1643336157728/Hierarchy+and+Differentiation+in+International+Regime+Complexes_Jan20.pdf

39 Galbreath, Härtel, and Wolff, cited above (Note 16).

40 Lamberto Zannier, "A Stronger OSCE for an Uncertain Future," in *OSCE Yearbook 2017*, ed. IFSH (Baden-Baden: Nomos, 2018), 35–50.

41 Thomas Greminger, "Strengthening Cooperative Security in Difficult Times: Three Years as Secretary General of the OSCE (2017–2020) – a Critical Appraisal," in *Multilateralism in Transition: Challenges and Opportunities for the OSCE*, eds. Simon J. A. Mason and Lisa Watanabe (Zürich: Center for Security Studies [CSS], ETH Zürich, 2021), 22–84.

42 Monika Wohlfeld and Fred Tanner, Comprehensive Security and New Challenges: Strengthening the OSCE (Rome: Istituto Affari Internazionali, 2021), p. 9, https://www.iai.it/sites/default/files/iaip2123.pdf

43 F. H. Hinsley, *Power and the Pursuit of Peace: Theory and Practice in the History of Relations Between States* (Cambridge: Cambridge University Press, 1963).

44 Stefanie Liechtenstein, "Ukraine Calls for Suspending Russia from the OSCE," *Security and Human Rights Monitor*, June 30, 2022, https://www.shrmonitor.org/ukraine-calls-to-expel-russia-from-the-osce/

45 Greminger, cited above (Note 41).

46 Byron Walfred Hunt, "The League of Nations and the Italo-Ethiopian Conflict" (master's thesis, University of Montana, 1957), iii, https://scholarworks.umt.edu/cgi/viewcontent.cgi?article=9685&context=etd

47 Eilstrup-Sangiovanni, "Death of International Organizations" and "What Kills International Organisations?," cited above (Note 1).

An Intractable Partner: Whither the OSCE's Relations with Turkmenistan?

*Luca Anceschi**

Abstract

This paper surveys the OSCE's relations with Turkmenistan. By detailing how the OSCE has engaged with its most authoritarian participating State, its findings contribute to debates on the viability of the current international order and the OSCE's relevance in the global community. Concluding with three interrelated policy recommendations, the paper argues that Turkmen-OSCE relations are marked by a minimum level of engagement and the marginalization of issues concerned with human rights and good governance.

Keywords
Turkmenistan, OSCE, authoritarianism, good governance promotion

To cite this publication: Luca Anceschi, "An Intractable Partner: Whither the OSCE's Relations with Turkmenistan?," in *OSCE Insights*, eds. Cornelius Friesendorf and Argyro Kartsonaki (Baden-Baden: Nomos, 2023), https://doi.org/10.5771/9783748933625-04

Introduction

On July 7, 2022, in co-operation with the Ministry of Foreign Affairs of Turkmenistan, the OSCE Centre in Ashgabat hosted a half-day event to mark the thirtieth anniversary of the establishment of Turkmen-OSCE relations. Speaking at the event, Turkmenistan's long-term foreign minister, Rashid Meredov, highlighted his country's unwavering commitment to "fruitful co-operation with the Organization for Security and Co-operation in Europe in strengthening security in the OSCE region."[1] In his remarks to guests and delegates attending the conference, the head of the Centre, Ambassador John MacGregor, noted the deepening of comprehensive co-operation between the parties, listing an expansive range of policy areas in which the relationship had returned substantive outcomes.[2]

Despite the optimism that permeated these assessments of Turkmen-OSCE co-operation, however, a closer look at bilateral interactions between Turkmenistan and the OSCE in the post-Soviet era suggests a different picture. Through interviews with OSCE officials and analysis of official documents issued by the OSCE and

* Luca Anceschi
Central & East European Studies,
The University of Glasgow
Luca.Anceschi@glasgow.ac.uk

the government of Turkmenistan, I will argue that, thirty years since their establishment, Turkmen-OSCE relations are marked by a minimum level of engagement and the avoidance of discussing thorny co-operation issues concerning human rights and good governance promotion.

I argue that this minimal engagement is viewed by both Turkmenistan and the OSCE as optimal in terms of the functioning of their broader relationship. In addition, the paper's findings are relevant to wider debates on the apparent hollowness and inadequacy of the current international order and the future of the OSCE as the Organization prepares to mark its fiftieth anniversary.[3]

In the following, I first analyze the parameter-setting work completed during the Niyazov era (1992–2006), when the OSCE and the Turkmen government established the rules of engagement governing their relationship. My focus then shifts to the long presidency of Gurbanguly Berdimuhamedov (2007–2022), in particular to co-operation between Turkmenistan and the OSCE in the human dimension, the field activities of the OSCE Centre in Ashgabat, and progress made in the OSCE's other two dimensions of security. I conclude by offering recommendations for future OSCE policy lines.

Setting the rules of engagement: Turkmen-OSCE relations in the Niyazov era

Throughout the post-Soviet era, successive Turkmen regimes pursued a deliberately isolationist foreign policy in which engagement with other nations was predicated on its contribution to preserving domestic power. Active participation in regional and international forms of multilateralism, including the OSCE, was no exception. It is through this lens that the dynamics governing relations between Turkmenistan and the OSCE should be viewed.

In July 1992, recognition of the Helsinki Final Act represented a default foreign policy option for the newly independent Turkmenistan. Rather than stemming from a principled "vision of the future" (as one of the last policy documents of the Niyazov era proclaimed), OSCE participation was in some sense an accidental development.[4] Saparmurat Niyazov's long, mercurial tenure oversaw the establishment of a collaborative pattern in which co-operation between the OSCE and Turkmenistan hinged on economic and environmental issues, with virtually no progress on the OSCE's mandate in the human dimension. Two landmark events defined Turkmen-OSCE relations when Niyazov was in power, contributing equally to consolidating the pattern described above.

On July 23, 1998, a decision issued by the OSCE Permanent Council established the OSCE Centre in Ashgabat, setting the mandate for a field presence the relevance and remit of which, as I will argue in greater detail below, developed in line with the evolution of the relationship between the OSCE and Turkmenistan.[5] Writing in 2001, Bess Brown noted that Turkmen officials were somewhat surprised by the Centre's engagement with the human dimension and were displeased with its ongoing efforts to build a civil society across Turkmenistan.[6] These remarks suggest that, at least in its early stages, the Centre did put a premium on human dimension activities—a focus that, as of this writing, seems to have lost much, if not all, of its impetus.

The second event that defined Turkmen-OSCE relations in the Niyazov era was the launch of the Moscow Mechanism to investigate the brutal wave of repression following the alleged coup of November 2002. OSCE investigations led by Emmanuel Decaux concluded in a detailed report that offered sixteen recommendations for improving governance in Turkmenistan, building on intensive in-country work and thorough engagement with local players.[7] The OSCE's sharpest criticism of Turkmenistan's human rights record to date, this report aimed to exert precisely the kind of pressure that the policy of "positive neutrality" was designed to contain.[8] The regime's imperviousness to the observations and recommendations voiced in the report revealed Turkmenistan as an intractable partner, instigating a collaborative pattern in which the human dimension was relegated to the margins in interactions between the regime in Ashgabat, the OSCE's institutions, and its field operations. In his report, Decaux noted that "Turkmenistan cannot constitute a 'black hole' within the OSCE" as far as the protection of human rights and respect for the rule of law are concerned.[9] Decaux's words would nevertheless prove prophetic: almost twenty years since the report's publication, and despite three decades of engagement with the OSCE, not only is Turkmenistan's record in governance one of the poorest across the entire OSCE area, but it is no longer part of the agenda pursued by the OSCE in its dealings with Turkmenistan.

Human dimension co-operation as a box-ticking exercise

During the long presidency of Gurbanguly Berdimuhamedov, Turkmenistan remained the most authoritarian of all OSCE participating States. Despite this, and at least superficially, the intensity of its co-operation with the OSCE did not decline. There is no reason to suppose that Serdar Berdimuhamedov's accession to the presidency in early 2022 will alter either Turkmenistan's rules of engagement with the OSCE or the quality of Turkmen governance.

A closer look at the electoral observation missions deployed by the OSCE Office for Democratic Institutions and Human Rights (ODIHR) in Turkmenistan reveals the pitfalls of the patterns of human dimension co-operation established in the Berdimuhamedov era. On the one hand, Turkmenistan has never wavered in its commitment to inviting OSCE/ODIHR observers to assess its electoral processes: the ODIHR online archive confirms that a report has indeed been filed after every Turkmen election.[10] On the other hand, personnel involved in these electoral observation missions have noted the essentially cosmetic nature of their remit. Although officially invited by the Turkmen government to participate in election observation, members of Needs Assessment Missions (NAMs) and Election Assessment Missions (EAMs) found themselves restricted to "inhibited forms of observation" once in Turkmenistan.[11] In particular, they were denied unrestricted and unsupervised access to candidates, media operators, and election officials and were prevented from performing other independent electoral observation activities.[12] The 2022 presidential election put this pattern into even greater relief: the Turkmen government's delay in extending its invitation to ODIHR restricted the latter's capacity to organize and deploy a full-fledged observation mission.[13] As a consequence, the vote that led to Serdar Berdimuhamedov's election was not observed by the OSCE/ODIHR, whose activities were limited to a small NAM that operated remotely.[14]

The government's flawed understanding of the mechanics of electoral observation surfaced yet again as part of the restricted activities of the 2022 NAM: ODIHR officials were reportedly asked for assistance with voting technology and voting accessibility for those with disabilities.[15] While prior ODIHR reports on Turkmen elections had emphasized the latter issue, noting that Turkmenistan was an outlier regarding voting rights for disabled individuals, the government in Ashgabat opted not to act on their recommendations until two weeks before the 2022 vote, indicating a lack of engagement with the human dimension mandate of the OSCE.[16]

It is against this background that the dysfunctional nature of OSCE-Turkmen co-operation in the human dimension comes more clearly into view: ODIHR reports have consistently noted the poor quality of Turkmenistan's electoral practices and have made elaborate recommendations, even offering direct assistance. Following the path established in the Niyazov era, the Berdimuhamedov regime deliberately ignored these recommendations and continued to hold essentially undemocratic elections, revealing a purely formalist understanding of the electoral process and the instrument of election observation.

Given Turkmenistan's failure to implement any of the recommendations articulated by successive ODIHR missions thus far, it is reasonable to ask why ODIHR continues to be involved in such an unfruitful partnership. In the eyes of many officials interviewed while researching this paper, although it remains an entirely inconsequential endeavor at present, the deployment of observation missions represents the one remaining instrument for preserving ongoing dialogue with Turkmenistan on electoral issues, especially since this matter has been conspicuously absent from the remit of the OSCE Centre in Ashgabat. In the electoral realm, any synergy that once existed between the Turkmen government and OSCE institutions and field missions fell apart in the 2010s, contributing to the further exclusion of the human dimension from the OSCE-Turkmenistan agenda.

The limits of field engagement: The OSCE Centre in Ashgabat

At the end of 2021, the OSCE Centre in Ashgabat—the field mission that spearheads the OSCE agenda in Turkmenistan—hosted six international staff members and employed twenty-three domestic personnel, a staffing level that has remained constant since 2014.[17] A similar picture of stability emerges from the funding structure for the Centre's activities: annual contributions from the OSCE Unified Budget remained at the €1.5–1.6 million mark from 2015 to 2021 and amounted to €1,661,200 for 2021. A set of more intriguing conclusions can be drawn by delving into the Centre's extrabudgetary expenses, captured graphically in the figure below.

OSCE Centre in Ashgabat: Extrabudgetary expenditure (in euros, 2015–2021)

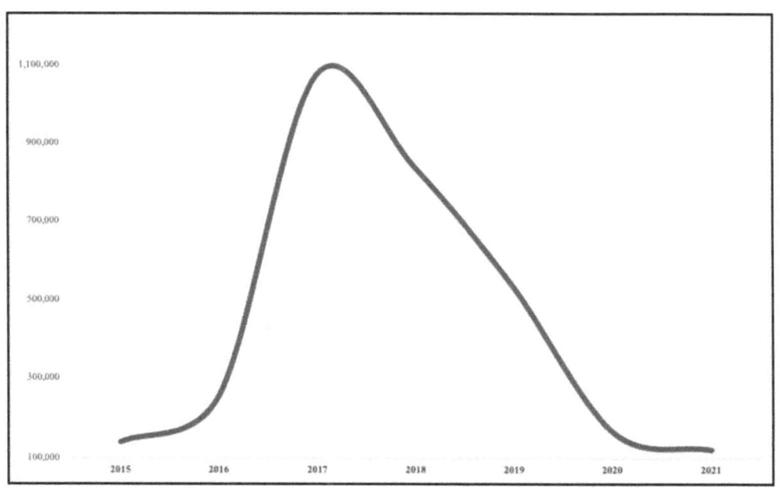

Presenting official OSCE data, the figure confirms that at the end of the period in question, the Centre in Ashgabat's extrabudgetary expenditure was the same as that reported for 2015.[18] The COVID-19 pandemic certainly accelerated the post-2017 declining trend, but the data for 2019 suggest that the reported expenditure for that year (€527,633) was effectively half the amount reached in 2017.

Extrabudgetary expenditure reflects the financial contributions made by participating States for projects that advance the OSCE agenda in Turkmenistan. The list of projects carried out in a specific calendar year (which is not publicly disclosed by the Centre) represents the outcome of a complex negotiation process.[19] There are many stakeholders in this process: the Centre's leadership, which identifies operational priorities that are likely to receive financial backing from OSCE participating States, individual participating States (or groups of States) that may elect to support specific projects in discrete policy areas, and, perhaps most importantly, the host country, whose preferences determine the parameters within which the project list can expand.

In personal communications, officials have confirmed the precariousness of this process, noting that the Centre's projects must reconcile different agendas in order to receive funding.[20] For instance, recently funded projects have had to bring together the Centre's ongoing focus on border security—in particular, on Turkmenistan's border with Afghanistan—and the OSCE's women's empowerment agenda. Further constraints on project selection stem from the intractability of the Turkmen regime when it comes to measures aimed at political liberalization and promotion of the rule of law. Keeping relations between the Centre and the host authorities positive has thus far required avoiding decisive action in the human dimension; projects funded through extra-budgetary contributions are no exception in this regard.

As the pandemic has slowly relented, the number of projects implemented by the OSCE Centre in Ashgabat has risen, yet pragmatic considerations have caused the Centre to shift its focus away from the human dimension.[21] This inconvenient truth tends to be downplayed in the annual communications from the Head of Mission to the OSCE Permanent Council regarding the Centre's activities.[22] While these documents are not accessible to the public, this can be inferred from the often positive assessments of human dimension co-operation voiced in participating States' official reactions to the director's report.[23]

The Centre's declining emphasis on the human dimension can also be deduced from the disappearance, in recent editions of the OSCE Annual Report, of transparent data on the provision of legal assistance to Turkmen citizens. This information is omitted from the 2020 and 2021 reports, whereas we know that in 2012 and 2013 the OSCE Centre in Ashgabat assisted 142 and 137 Turkmen citizens, respectively, in human rights cases.[24] While it was a key concern during the Centre's early operations,[25] co-operation in the human dimension is now ostensibly absent from its public remit and likely represents a marginal consideration in those segments of the Centre's agenda that are not usually disclosed to the public.

Like ODIHR's electoral remit in Turkmenistan, the activities of the OSCE Centre in Ashgabat have been affected by what we might call the *tyranny of engagement*. Given the tightrope it has had to walk, the Centre may have had no choice but to resort to lowest-common-denominator policies in its efforts to reconcile budgetary constraints with Turkmenistan's unwillingness to tolerate pressure regarding rule of law reform. Relevant OSCE officials have suggested that when it comes to assessing the success of the Centre's activities, even an apparently ineffective field presence is preferable to no in-country presence at all. As one official shared, "without a field presence there will be no future change."[26] Yet opportunities for future change are only available in those policy areas on which OSCE fieldwork focuses more directly. In the case of Turkmenistan, where collaboration in the human dimension is limited, the Centre's work may only make progress in less controversial policy realms.

Baby steps at thirty: What is the OSCE actually doing in Turkmenistan?

OSCE officials have devoted much of their attention in Turkmenistan to securing the country's porous and generally unstable border with Afghanistan.[27] Initiatives such as the 2015 training course for eighteen officers from the State Border Service of Turkmenistan and the 2018 joint workshop for senior border officials from both Turkmenistan and Afghanistan show that this policy area was on the OSCE's radar even in the prepandemic years.[28] Both initiatives were funded through the Centre's extrabudgetary projects.

The securitization of the Turkmen-Afghan border could also take on a distinctly environmental dimension in the future. As the ENVSEC Initiative—of which the OSCE is a key partner—has observed, the intersection of chronic instability and climate change may lead to the further deterioration of security in this border region.[29] Personal communications with relevant officials confirm that matters of environmental consideration are likely to constitute a future area of concern for the OSCE in Turkmenistan.[30]

A declared commitment to including Turkmenistan in connectivity networks both within and beyond Central Asia represents another significant item on the agenda being pursued locally by the OSCE. With that said, this policy focus remains aspirational at best. Recent work on economic diplomacy in the OSCE area does not identify Turkmenistan as a developing connectivity hub.[31] Moreover, media reports on Turkmen affairs confirm that, both prior to and following the pandemic, the regime in Ashgabat has maintained its idiosyncratic attitude *vis-à-vis* connectivity and regional integration.[32]

Conclusion and recommendations

The findings of this paper corroborate some of the key conclusions advanced by prior scholarship on the OSCE's role in, and impact on, Central Asia. To begin with, the observed trend of excluding human dimension measures from the OSCE agenda in Turkmenistan confirms Maria Debre's conclusions regarding the institutionalization of "non-interventionist norms that shield regimes from unwanted external interference into politically sensitive areas of domestic politics."[33] Acquiescence to this sanitized interactive model is a pattern that has also been identified by Alexander Warkotsch, who notes that a lack of visible incentives to introduce human dimension reforms has led authoritarian leaders across the OSCE area—including Turkmenistan—to regard OSCE-sponsored liberalization measures as a direct threat to their authoritarian stability.[34]

This paper has also shown that failure to regard authoritarian politics as a source of insecurity, while it may preserve a minimum degree of engagement with Turkmenistan, is likely only to advance the OSCE on its inexorable "path towards irrelevancy"—to borrow a phrase from Karolina Kluczewska.[35] Turkmenistan's potential for instability remains significant precisely because of the authoritarian governance patterns that OSCE officials have thus far left unaddressed: the food/energy nexus—wherein the kleptocratic management of Turkmen gas revenues has led to the rise of food insecurity across the country—is a vivid example of how authoritarian entrenchment has facilitated the deterioration of the population's human security.[36]

Co-operation that ignores the human dimension ultimately erodes the relevance of the OSCE *acquis* and its most fundamental normative documents, as William Hill has argued.[37] In addition to being detrimental to Turkmenistan's security, these engagement patterns continue to constrain the role played by the OSCE as the global community becomes less democratic.

My analysis points to three policy lines that could be adopted as part of the OSCE agenda in Turkmenistan:

1. Encourage further scrutiny of the Turkmen regime's human rights record, for example by encouraging the OSCE Centre in Ashgabat to offer greater and more visible assistance to Turkmen citizens persecuted by the regime.
2. Refuse to engage in window-dressing election observation, for example by demanding that observation missions be given timely notification of upcoming elections and fair, unfettered access to voting procedures.
3. Promote human rights as a fundamental element of the OSCE security framework, for example by negotiating the inclusion of human dimension projects on the list of the OSCE Centre in Ashgabat's extrabudgetary activities.

Notes

1 OSCE, "OSCE and Turkmenistan Mark 30 Years of Co-operation," July 8, 2022, https://www.osce.org/centre-in-ashgabat/522316

2 Turkmen official media reproduced lengthy excerpts of MacGregor's speech in: Irina Imankulieva, "30 лет успешного сотрудничества," *Neytral'nii Turkmenistan*, July 8, 2022, 3.

3 Philip Zelikow, "The Hollow Order: Rebuilding an International System That Works," *Foreign Affairs* 101, no. 4 (July/August 2022): 107–19; William H. Hill, "The OSCE Approaching Fifty: Does the Organization Have a Future?," in *OSCE Insights*, eds. Cornelius Friesendorf and Argyro Kartsonaki (Baden-Baden: Nomos, 2023), https://doi.org/10.5771/9783748933625-01

4 Delegation of Turkmenistan to the OSCE, Statement by the Head of Delegation of Turkmenistan at 14th Meeting of the OSCE Ministerial Council, MC.DEL/37/06 (Brussels: December 4, 2006), https://www.osce.org/files/f/documents/5/9/22862.pdf

5 OSCE Permanent Council, Decision No. 244, PC.DEC/244 (July 23, 1998), https://www.osce.org/files/f/documents/c/a/40139.pdf

6 Bess Brown, "Turkmenistan and the OSCE," in *OSCE Yearbook 2001*, ed. IFSH (Baden-Baden: Nomos, 2002), 107, https://ifsh.de/file-CORE/documents/yearbook/english/01/Brown.pdf

7 Emmanuel Decaux, OSCE Rapporteur's Report on Turkmenistan, ODIHR.GAL/15/03 (March 12, 2003), https://www.osce.org/files/f/documents/0/5/18372.pdf

8 Luca Anceschi, *Turkmenistan's Foreign Policy: Positive Neutrality and the Consolidation of the Turkmen Regime* (London-New York: Routledge, 2008), 128–37.

9 Decaux, cited above (Note 7), 3.

10 OSCE/ODIHR, "Elections in Turkmenistan," https://www.osce.org/odihr/elections/turkmenistan

11 OSCE official, personal communication with the author, May 2022.

12 OSCE/ODIHR, Turkmenistan Presidential Election 12 February 2017—OSCE/ODIHR Election Assessment Mission Final Report (Warsaw: May 10, 2017), https://www.osce.org/files/f/documents/b/1/316586.pdf

13 The OSCE received an invitation to conduct the NAM on February 23 and an invitation to observe the election on February 25. The vote was scheduled for March 12, 2022.

14 One OSCE official (cited above, Note 11) confirmed that different monitoring organizations were treated differently regarding exemptions to the strict COVID-19 quarantine regimen enforced in Turkmenistan in early 2022. Unlike observers from the Commonwealth of Independent States and the Shanghai Cooperation Organisation, who were promptly included in this exemption system, ODIHR members were not guaranteed quarantine-free travel to Turkmenistan up until a few days before the deployment of the NAM—a move that forced it to be downgraded to a remote mission and that led the ODIHR leadership to decide against the deployment of a full observation mission on election day. This difference in treatment is also highlighted by Deirdre Brown, deputy head of the UK delegation to the OSCE, in her response to the 2022 report by the head of the OSCE Centre in Ashgabat, https://www.gov.uk/government/speeches/report-by-osce-head-of-centre-in-ashgabat-uk-response-june-2022

15 OSCE official, personal communication with the author, May 2022.

16 Recommendation #13 listed in the 2017 EAM Report (cited above, Note 12, 18) explicitly mentioned the systematic "disenfranchisement of persons with mental disabilities" as one of the main obstacles to voter registration in Turkmenistan. The same theme is also frequently touched on in a subsequent report: OSCE/ODIHR, Turkmenistan Parliamentary Elections 25 March 2018—OSCE/ODIHR Election Assessment Mission Final Report (Warsaw: May 30, 2018), 1, 5, 7, 14, https://www.osce.org/files/f/documents/2/8/382915_0.pdf

17 Data on the Centre's staffing size can be retrieved in different editions of the OSCE Annual Report, https://www.osce.org/annual-reports

18 Data on funding for the Centre's activities can be retrieved in different editions of the OSCE Annual Report, cited above (Note 17).

19 See, for instance, OSCE, Annual Report 2021 (Vienna: 2022), 55–56, https://www.osce.org/files/f/documents/a/4/520912.pdf

20 OSCE official, personal communication with the author, September 2022.

21 In 2021, the Centre reported a 33 percent increase in the total number of projects funded from the 2020 baseline of 44.

22 OSCE official, personal communication with the author, September 2022.

23 "We also welcome the Centre's work in the third dimension, especially in promoting media freedom and enhancing the capacity of the Ombudsperson," Permanent Delegation of Norway to the OSCE, "Statement in Response to the Head of the OSCE Centre in Ashgabat," June 17, 2021, https://www.norway.no/en/missions/osce/norway-and-the-osce/statements/norwegian-statements-2021/statement-in-response-to-the-head-of-the-osce-centre-in-ashgabat/

24 OSCE, Annual Report 2012 (Vienna: 2013), 58, https://www.osce.org/files/f/documents/2/2/100193.pdf. Data for 2013 are retrievable at: OSCE, Annual Report 2013 (Vienna: 2013), 74, https://www.osce.org/files/f/documents/7/4/116947.pdf

25 Brown, cited above (Note 6), 110.

26 OSCE official, personal communication with the author, September 2022.

27 OSCE officials, personal communication with the author, September 2022. Frequent mention of border management is also made in the sections on the OSCE Centre in Ashgabat's activities in post-2019 editions of the OSCE Annual Report.

28 OSCE, "OSCE Trains Turkmenistan Border Guards in Border Management and Threat Assessment," April 29, 2015, https://www.osce.org/ashgabat/154276; OSCE Centre in Ashgabat, "Border Management," https://www.osce.org/centre-in-ashgabat/106253

29 ENVSEC Initiative, Climate Change and Security: Central Asia, https://www.osce.org/files/f/documents/5/8/331991.pdf

30 OSCE official, personal communication with the author, September 2022.

31 Stefan Wolff, Economic Diplomacy and Connectivity: What Role for the OSCE? (Birmingham: Institute for Conflict, Cooperation and Security at the University of Birmingham, 2018), https://www.birmingham.ac.uk/Documents/college-social-sciences/government-society/iccs/news-events/2018/Osce-Report.pdf; Stefan Wolff, Anastasiya Bayok, Rahimullah Kakar, and Niva Yau, The OSCE and Central Asia: Options for Engagement in the Context of the Crisis in Afghanistan and the War in Ukraine (Birmingham, Hamburg, Vienna: OSCE Network of Think Tanks and Academic Institutions, 2022).

32 On some matters, Turkmenistan wants to join the rest of the world. On others, it wants the opposite: "Turkmenistan: Shining City at a Foothill," *Ahal-Teke: A Turkmenistan Bulletin*, September 20, 2022, https://eurasianet.org/turkmenistan-shining-city-at-a-foothill

33 Maria J. Debre, "Clubs of Autocrats: Regional Organizations and Authoritarian Survival," *Review of International Organizations* 17, no. 3 (2022): 504.

34 Alexander Warkotsch, "The OSCE as an Agent of Socialisation? International Norm Dynamics and Political Change in Central Asia," *Europe-Asia Studies* 59, no. 5 (2007): 844.

35 Karolina Kluczewska, "Benefactor, Industry or Intruder? Perceptions of International Organizations in Central Asia—the Case of the OSCE in Tajikistan," *Central Asian Survey* 36, no. 3 (2017): 368.

36 Luca Anceschi, "Nahrungsmittelunsicherheit, Armut und autoritärer Zerfall in Turkmenistan," *Zentralasien-Analysen* 143 (September 30, 2020): 9–12.

37 Hill, cited above (Note 3), 9.

Beyond Muddling Through: Towards an OSCE Interim Approach

*Wolfgang Zellner**

Abstract

The Russian aggression against Ukraine represents a complete negation of everything for which the OSCE stands: a rules-based order, co-operative security, respect for state sovereignty, and the inviolability of borders. This raises the question as to whether the OSCE can exist and work in a political environment that contradicts its very *raison d'être*. This paper briefly outlines three factors that will likely determine the future of the Organization. Against this background, it presents an OSCE interim approach for the next three years and recommendations for areas of activity.

Keywords
OSCE, strategy, Ukraine, war

To cite this publication: Wolfgang Zellner, "Beyond Muddling Through: Towards an OSCE Interim Approach," in *OSCE Insights*, eds. Cornelius Friesendorf and Argyro Kartsonaki (Baden-Baden: Nomos, 2023), https://doi.org/10.5771/9783748933625-05

Introduction

The basic principles on which the OSCE is structured entail a rules-based order, co-operative security, respect for the sovereignty of states, and the inviolability of their borders. The Russian invasion of Ukraine in February 2022 violated all these commitments. Consequently, a large majority of OSCE participating States have ceased co-operation with the Russian Federation and are asking themselves whether this should also include ending joint decision-making in the OSCE.

The OSCE therefore finds itself in an existential crisis. The overarching question is whether the OSCE can exist and work in a political environment that contradicts its very *raison d'être*. This paper seeks to answer this question by presenting a strategy for the OSCE—something that the Organization has always been missing.[1] It argues that the OSCE should be ready to resort to informal modes of running the Organization for the time being, replacing formal decision-making where necessary.

Finding a proper answer to the crucial questions of whether and how the OSCE can play a productive role in Euro-

* Wolfgang Zellner
Institute for Peace Research and Security Policy at the University of Hamburg (IFSH)
zellner@ifsh.de

pean security policy requires an assessment of broader political developments. "Wait and see" attitudes and "muddling through" approaches, frequently used by the Organization, are inadequate. This paper briefly presents three factors that will determine the OSCE's future as an international security organization. It then argues that the OSCE can overcome the "consensus trap"[2] by opting for informal decision-making procedures. The paper concludes with recommendations for a three-year interim strategy that focuses on political issues and aims to leave as many options open as possible.

Three factors shaping the future of the OSCE

The OSCE's future as a consensus-based organization will likely depend on the following three factors: the duration and outcome of the war in Ukraine, Russia's decreased strength and influence, and the speed and outcome of the EU accession process of the Western Balkans and Ukraine.

First, the outcome of the war in Europe will determine the OSCE's room for maneuver. It is unclear how long the war in Ukraine will continue, and experts fundamentally disagree on its likely outcome.[3] Equally unclear is what type of ceasefire or peace agreement will ultimately be adopted to terminate the war. One possibility is an unstable ceasefire agreement that constitutes an interim stage until the next round of war. The other possibility is a stable peace agreement that includes a ceasefire, a territorial accord, and guarantees. Depending on the outcome, the OSCE's political room for maneuver could either increase or decrease. It will likely decrease in the case of an unstable ceasefire and increase if a more comprehensive peace agreement is achieved and a more co-operative environment is established. In any case, the basic confrontational constellation between Russia and the West will remain in force until a favorable regime change of some sort occurs in the Russian Federation. But this is well beyond the horizon.

Second, the aggression against Ukraine has weakened Russia in every respect: politically, economically, militarily, and in terms of its ability to control its so-called "near abroad"—in institutional terms, the members of the Collective Security Treaty Organization (CSTO). Recent developments have exposed Russia's weaknesses: In September 2022, Armenian and Azerbaijani forces clashed, resulting in the death of about 200 soldiers. Soon after, Kyrgyz and Tajik forces began fighting, resulting in dozens of casualties. The Russian-led CSTO had nothing to offer but an observer mission and a call for peace. Russia's shrinking influence in the South Caucasus and Central Asia has opened up co-operative options for the OSCE, provided these states are interested in increased OSCE activity. At the same time, conflict potentials in these regions that were hitherto suppressed by the Russian Federation may now escalate. Thus, there is a new need for conflict prevention and management initiatives. The question is whether the OSCE can perform these tasks.

Third, some of the remaining non-EU Balkan states and Ukraine may approach and join the EU sooner than expected. This means that these states will fall within the sphere of competence of the EU, resulting in less need for OSCE activities. Russia's shrinking sphere of influence and EU expansion will result in an even clearer bipolar structure in Europe, with sharper dividing lines and fewer states lying in between. For the OSCE, this will mean less political room for maneuver.

Overcoming the "consensus trap"

According to Fred Tanner, one of the OSCE's weaknesses is what he calls the "consensus trap": "Russia, but also other countries, [...] have used the refusal of consensus as [a] veto on agenda-setting, budget, reform efforts, crisis decision-making and this often as a bargaining chip on quarrels not related at all to the matters at stake."[4] Over the years, while it was difficult to work with this kind of trap, it was possible—albeit with great losses in terms of policy coherence and efficiency. Since the Russian invasion of Ukraine, however, it has been impossible to reach consensus. There are two options for dealing with the impasse created by this lack of consensus: either suspend Russia's participation in the OSCE based on the consensus-minus-one rule or bypass Russia's veto power by running the OSCE's policy operations on a more informal basis, governed by the Chairperson and the Troika.

The consensus-minus-one rule was formulated in the conclusions of the 1992 Prague Meeting of the Council of Ministers:

> The Council decided, in order to develop further the CSCE's capability to safeguard human rights, democracy and the rule of law through peaceful means, that appropriate action may be taken by the Council or the Committee of Senior Officials, if necessary in the absence of the consent of the State concerned, in cases of clear, gross, and uncorrected violations of relevant CSCE commitments.[5]

This stipulation has been used only once, on July 8, 1992, when the thirteenth meeting of the Committee of Senior Officials suspended Serbia and Montenegro from participating in the 1992 Helsinki Summit.[6] This suspension remained in force until November 7, 2000, when the former Republic of Yugoslavia rejoined the OSCE. Could the OSCE apply the same approach to Russia now? The suspension of the Russian Federation would be justified. The Russian aggression against Ukraine clearly represents a "clear, gross, and uncorrected" violation of OSCE commitments. The case looks different from a political point of view, however. It is doubtful whether a consensus-minus-one suspension decision against Russia could even be reached, as this would require the collaboration of Belarus and the other members of the Russian-led CSTO.

The other option, should attempts to reach consensus with Russia fail, is to run the OSCE on a more informal basis by applying an informal consensus-minus-one rule. This should be possible, as the OSCE has always been a highly informal communication network in its day-to-day business. This approach would require much consultation and discipline among the participating States, as well as strong leadership by the Chair and the Troika. Such a governance scheme would necessarily involve agreement on a budget, a Secretary General and heads of institutions, the continuation of at least some field operations, and, last and most difficult, a Chairpersonship.

Let us start with the budget. For the past few years, the adoption of the Unified Budget has generally not taken place until the summer; thus, the OSCE is already used to working with provisional budgets. The disadvantage of a provisional budget is that money can only be spent along already existing program and project lines; new projects must be funded by voluntary contributions. Should provisional budgeting come to an end, the same would be true of the entire budget: all funding would need to come from voluntary contributions. This would show Russia and other states that blocking the budget is no longer the sharp weapon it used to be. But again, such an approach requires great discipline, particularly among the larger Western participating States. If they do not provide the funds, everything will quickly come to an end.

The OSCE institutions—the Office for Democratic Institutions and Human Rights (ODIHR), the High Commissioner on National Minorities (HCNM), and the Representative on Freedom of the Media (RFoM)—should be continued at any rate, as should the field operations, as far as the host state agrees. As Jos Boonstra has suggested, one "way to do this is decoupling the OSCE decision-making bodies [...] from the rest of the structures, missions, and bodies."[7] Thus, the institutions would be led as Chairperson projects with budgets based on voluntary contributions. The same would apply to field operations. The field operations' mandates were eventually extended at the end of 2022, apart from those related to Ukraine. However, as it is unclear whether this exercise can be repeated in 2023, it is worthwhile to consider other, more informal options. For example, Ian Kelly, former head of the US OSCE delegation, proposed: "If the field missions' mandates are not reviewed this year, which many fear, the Chairperson-in-Office [...] can also use their authorities to maintain a type of field mission (for example, as an 'Office of the Special Representative of the CiO') in OSCE countries where the host supports their continuation. They can be funded by like-minded OSCE states."[8] The OSCE is already moving in this direction. In August 2022, the Chair and the Secretary General announced a support program for Ukraine, replacing the OSCE Project Co-ordinator in Ukraine, which was closed due to Russia's veto.[9]

While heads of missions are appointed by the Chair, things are more difficult when it comes to the heads of institutions, who are appointed by Ministerial Council decisions. The terms of office of Secretary General Helga Maria Schmid, the HCNM, the Director of ODIHR, and the RFoM expire in December 2023. At that point—comparable to the situation from July to December 2020, when all four posts were vacant—their formal or informal deputies will take over their duties in an acting capacity. There is no time limit for such a solution.

The only really difficult task consists in securing subsequent Chairpersonships. The 2023 OSCE Chair is North Macedonia, to be followed by Finland in 2025, fifty years after the Helsinki Final Act (HFA). The Chair for 2024 has yet to be elected, which leaves the task of bridging this gap to diplomatic innovation. Extending North Macedonia's Chairpersonship and giving a stronger role to the Troika might at least provide a partial solution.

The question is whether the more informal approach to running the OSCE sketched above is legitimate and feasible. Admittedly, such an approach would be a major affront to the Russian Federation and would have been unthinkable under "normal" conditions. With its aggression against Ukraine, however, Russia has forfeited any right to be treated on normal terms. The OSCE must not allow itself to be destroyed by Russia, which is itself destroying the civilian infrastructure of a major neighboring country—a campaign which, according to the Geneva Conventions, constitutes a serious war crime. If Russia does not like this kind of treatment in the OSCE, it is free to leave the Organization. However, Russia will likely avoid taking this step insofar as most of its CSTO allies would not follow suit, which would expose its isolation.

If the informal model is to be run successfully, the transformation from formal consensus to a more informal governance scheme must be taken seriously. This would require close consultation with even the smallest states on a wide range of issues. This kind of diligence can only help the Organization, however. In this sense, as it would require a tremendous amount of political will and discipline, the informal interim approach proposed here goes far beyond the usual strategy of muddling through.

Elements of an OSCE interim agenda: Recommendations

In what follows, I offer suggestions for a three-year OSCE work program focused on key political issues and aimed at leaving as many options open to the OSCE as possible. Nothing is preventing OSCE participating States from developing such an agenda. As Walter Kemp has argued, "[t]here is no need to have a consensus-based decision to launch such a process."[10] The process could start in an informal manner co-ordinated by the Chair and the Troika, with or without Russia's participation. The agenda should include the following items.

Inclusive dialogue with or without Russia. The basis of the CSCE/OSCE's work has always been unconditioned dialogue on any relevant European security issue. Russia should not be excluded from such a dialogue a priori; rather, one of the dialogue's aims should be to force Russia to explain its behavior, again and again. Just as it is important for President Macron and Chancellor Scholz to talk to President Putin, it is important to include the

Russian OSCE delegation in discussions. Walk-outs of the sort that occurred in the first months of Russia's aggression against Ukraine are unproductive. The security dialogue should focus on two issues: first, how to contain the Russian aggression while at the same time laying the foundations for a more co-operative European order; and second, regional security issues in areas where Russia's influence is decreasing, leaving a security vacuum in its wake.

Implementation of OSCE norms. For a norm-based organization like the OSCE, it is imperative that it continue to monitor and discuss the implementation of its commitments in all circumstances. First and foremost, this means safeguarding and continuing the work of ODIHR, the HCNM, and the RFoM. If either Russia or Belarus blocks the budgets for these institutions, they should be continued as Chairperson projects funded by voluntary contributions. The same is true for the Human Dimension Implementation Meeting (HDIM), which did not take place in 2020 due to COVID-19 and in 2021 due to lack of consensus. In an important move, the Polish Chair organized a Human Dimension Conference in September and October 2022, the format of which was similar to the HDIM.[11] In this context, the Russian Federation's ongoing grave violations of human rights should be raised regularly. Apart from the three institutions, the Permanent Council should be the central platform for discussing the implementation of OSCE norms and commitments.

Reaching out to the South Caucasus and Central Asia has become more important than ever. First, Russia's decreasing influence could lead to a flare-up of previously suppressed violent conflicts. Therefore, it is important that the OSCE strengthen its conflict prevention efforts in these regions. Second, China is already the most important trade partner of the Central Asian states and the ultimate guarantor of their sovereignty against possible Russian attack. It should not be allowed to fill the Central Asian security vacuum alone, however. Third, since Central Asia is not a key focus of the main Western organizations, the OSCE could play a leading role in this respect. However, it remains to be seen whether the participating States would endorse such a role and whether the Organization would be able to perform it properly.

Implementation of a future Russian-Ukrainian ceasefire agreement. The OSCE is not well suited to the role of mediator in the Russian-Ukrainian war. As William H. Hill has remarked, "[t]he OSCE is too large, unwieldy, and diverse to serve as a direct mediator in the conflict."[12] This is underlined by the OSCE's weak record in resolving even much smaller conflicts, such as the Karabakh conflict, where the so-called OSCE Minsk Group under the three Co-Chairs France, Russia, and the United States no longer plays a role. However, the OSCE should attempt to play a role in the implementation of a future ceasefire agreement, as it did from 2014 to 2022 with its Special Monitoring Mission (SMM) to Ukraine. Two aspects demand attention in this regard. First, in view of the gravity and global significance of the conflict, it would be preferable to have a UN mission based on a UN

Security Council mandate. At the same time, this would imply the acceptance of the mandate by Russia. Second, it should be kept in mind that neither Ukraine nor Russia welcomed the SMM and the OSCE's role in Ukraine, for different reasons. Nevertheless, the OSCE should try to contribute its extensive experience in the implementation of a future Russian-Ukrainian ceasefire agreement.

Arms control. It may sound surprising in the current circumstances, but as Alexander Mattelaer has rightly remarked, "[o]ver the longer term, the conclusion of the Russian war against Ukraine is likely to impose new requirements in terms of arms control."[13] This is true for several reasons. First, any durable ceasefire or peace agreement will contain elements of arms control (ceilings in certain areas, information exchange, verification). Second, a peace agreement will likely contain territorial provisions that satisfy neither Ukraine nor Russia. Consequently, "Ukraine needs guarantees that Russia will not try to move the borders using force once again in the future, while Russia needs guarantees that Ukraine will not go to war to try to resolve the territorial issue, regardless of who is in power in Kyiv."[14] Part of this will likely be provided by arms control regulations. Third, there will be a need for sub-regional arms control for regions such as the South Caucasus and parts of Central Asia. Because of this potential agenda, it is advisable to keep the Forum for Security Co-operation workable.

Using the fiftieth anniversary of the HFA to discuss the future of the Organization. The fiftieth anniversary of the HFA will provide an opportunity to convene an informal Ministerial Council or Summit meeting in Helsinki focused on taking stock of where things stand and discussing strategies for ensuring a brighter future. The three years leading up to such an event should be used to organize a broad discussion process including participating States, other international organizations, members of parliament, civil society leaders, and academics. If anyone can co-ordinate such a process, it is Finland.

It is unlikely that the OSCE will be able to implement all elements of such an agenda. It is the participating States who will decide on the Organization's future tasks and role. Nevertheless, it is worth attempting to address a meaningful agenda that keeps political options open.

Notes

1 Walter Kemp, "Ending Up Somewhere Else: The Need for Strategy in the OSCE," in *OSCE Insights*, eds. Cornelius Friesendorf and Argyro Kartsonaki (Baden-Baden: Nomos, 2023).

2 Fred Tanner, "The OSCE and European Security: Towards a Point of No Return?," in *Envisioning Peace in a Time of War: The New School of Multilateralism*, ed. Ursula Werther-Pietsch (Vienna: Facultas, 2022), 60.

3 The chairman of the US Joint Chiefs of Staff, General Mark Milley, said the following on November 16, 2022: "The probability of a Ukrainian military victory—defined as kicking the Russians out of all of Ukraine to include what they claim as Crimea—the probability of that happening anytime soon is not high, militarily." See "US-General: Baldiger Sieg

unwahrscheinlich," *ZDF*, November 17, 2022, https://www.zdf.de/nachrichten/politik/ukraine-russland-krieg-general-milley-usa-100.html. Much more optimistically, the Ukrainian deputy defense minister, General Wolodymyr Hawrylow, suggested that the war could be over by the end of spring 2023. He did not exclude an advance of Ukrainian forces to Crimea by the end of 2022 (see "Ukrainischer General: Krieg zum Frühlingsende vorbei," *NTV*, November 19, 2022, https://www.n-tv.de/politik/Ukrainischer-General-Krieg-zum-Fruehlingsende-vorbei-article23729746.html).

4 Tanner, cited above (Note 2), 60.

5 CSCE, Second Meeting of the Council, Summary of Conclusions, Prague Document on Further Development of OSCE Institutions and Structures, Declaration on Non-Proliferation and Arms Transfers (Prague: 1992), 16, https://www.osce.org/files/f/documents/7/b/40270.pdf

6 OSCE, "Serbia and Montenegro Suspended as a Participating State," July 8, 1992, https://www.osce.org/node/58332

7 Jos Boonstra, "The OSCE: Back to Square One?," in *Russia's War against Ukraine: Implications for the Future of the OSCE*, OSCE Network Perspectives I/2022, eds. Cornelius Friesendorf and Stefan Wolff (OSCE Network of Think Tanks and Academic Institutions, June 2022), 16, https://osce-network.net/fileadmin/user_upload/OSCE_Network_Perspectives_2022_20June_final.pdf

8 Ian Kelly, "Will the OSCE Devolve into the CSCE?," in *Russia's War against Ukraine: Implications for the Future of the OSCE*, OSCE Network Perspectives 1/2022, eds. Cornelius Friesendorf and Stefan Wolff (OSCE Network of Think Tanks and Academic Institutions, June 2022), 49, https://osce-network.net/fileadmin/user_upload/OSCE_Network_Perspectives_2022_20June_final.pdf

9 OSCE, "OSCE Chairman-in-Office and Secretary General Announce OSCE Support Programme for Ukraine," August 3, 2022, https://www.osce.org/Chairmanship/523754

10 Kemp, cited above (Note 1), 7.

11 OSCE, "Human Dimension Conference Concludes in Warsaw," October 7, 2022, https://www.osce.org/chairmanship/528399

12 William H. Hill, "The OSCE Approaching Fifty: Does the Organization Have a Future?," in *OSCE Insights*, eds. Cornelius Friesendorf and Argyro Kartsonaki (Baden-Baden: Nomos, 2023), 9.

13 Alexander Mattelaer, Keeping the OSCE Alive, Egmont Policy Brief 287 (Brussels: Egmont Institute, 2022), 3, https://www.egmontinstitute.be/app/uploads/2022/09/Alexander-Mattelaer_PolicyBrief287.pdf?type=pdf

14 Vladimir Frolov, "New Commander, New Goals for Russia in Ukraine," Carnegie Endowment for International Peace, November 1, 2022, https://carnegieendowment.org/politika/88301

The CSCE: Lessons from the Past

*Andrei Zagorski**

Abstract

Amid the several crises with which the Helsinki process was confronted during the last decade of the Cold War, various strategies were developed to keep it moving forward. These included, *inter alia*, keeping the agenda flexible, expanding it, and harnessing the asymmetry of the participating States' preferences by introducing the concept of balanced progress in all relevant dimensions of the CSCE. This enabled major stakeholders to maintain a strong feeling of co-ownership of the process, despite voices in both the East and the West that questioned the rationale of the Helsinki process. After discussing how these strategies were applied in the CSCE years, this paper concludes by exploring their contemporary relevance. In doing so, it elaborates on both the differences and the similarities between the CSCE and the OSCE, such as the clearly asymmetric preferences of their participating States.

Keywords

European security, CSCE, Helsinki process, OSCE, human rights

To cite this publication: Andrei Zagorski, "The CSCE: Lessons from the Past," in *OSCE Insights*, eds. Cornelius Friesendorf and Argyro Kartsonaki (Baden-Baden: Nomos, 2023), https://doi.org/10.5771/9783748933625-06

Introduction

The crisis the OSCE is facing is not the first in its history. It is not even its first existential crisis, although it may be its gravest thus far. As early as February 1974, only a few months into the second stage of the Conference on Security and Co-operation in Europe (CSCE) and following the arrest of Alexander Solzhenitsyn, "the Conference held its breath," its fate dependent on how Solzhenitsyn was treated in Moscow.[1] Just a few years later, the debate over human rights nearly brought the first follow-up meeting in Belgrade (1977–1978) to the point of collapse. The opening of the second follow-up meeting in Madrid (1980–1983) was overshadowed by the Soviet intervention in Afghanistan, and in early 1982 the meeting was suspended for several months following the introduction of martial law in Poland in December 1981. Against this backdrop, the

* Andrei Zagorski
Primakov National Research Institute of World Economy and International Relations (IMEMO), Russian Academy of Sciences, Moscow
zagorskiandrei@gmail.com

very continuity of the Helsinki process could not be taken for granted. Frustrated with the degeneration of subsequent meetings into an arena of mutual blaming and shaming rather than substantive discussions amid resumed confrontation, the Soviet Union and the United States repeatedly considered withdrawing from the CSCE.

Public discussion of the Soviet human rights record at the Belgrade Meeting strengthened the voices of those in Moscow who opposed the Helsinki process. Preparing for the Madrid Meeting, the Soviet Union called into question the value of continuing the CSCE process should the West resume Belgrade-type polemics.[2] The delegations in Madrid "wondered whether the Soviets had come to Madrid to put an end to a diplomatic enterprise that had ceased to benefit them and brought only disappointment."[3]

During the 1980 presidential campaign, Ronald Reagan questioned why US diplomats should go to Madrid when American athletes were boycotting the Moscow Olympics. Several Western states, in particular the United States, France, and Denmark, suggested postponing the meeting.[4] Following the introduction of martial law in Poland in December 1981, the United States insisted that the meeting should not resume after the winter break.[5] This would have resulted in the termination of the CSCE process.

As East-West tensions grew in the 1980s, Western criticism of the CSCE grew as well. The 1985 Helsinki Ministerial Meeting, which was meant to commemorate the tenth anniversary of the Final Act, was marked by a gloomy atmosphere. Frustration with the lack of progress in the human dimension strengthened the voices of those in the West who held that the rationale of détente and the original Helsinki trade-offs were based on false assumptions about the thinking of the Soviet leaders. In 1986, the US government considered renouncing the Helsinki Accords and explored practical ways to do so.[6]

Nevertheless, the CSCE survived. The reasons for this were manifold. Apart from the advocacy of a number of participating States (who opposed criticism of the Helsinki Accords by pointing to their long-term effects) and the mediation provided by the group of neutral and non-aligned states, the participating States developed a number of strategies that enabled the CSCE to move forward. These included harnessing the diversity of the participating States' interests by pursuing *asymmetric bargaining*; understanding the CSCE as a *process* based on a modus vivendi agreement that anticipated forthcoming change; making the most of its broad, flexible agenda to ensure *balanced progress* across the various baskets (dimensions), thus reflecting the asymmetric preferences of the participating States; and *elaborating on those Helsinki provisions* that generated the most controversy in order to reduce their ambiguity.

This paper traces the application of these strategies up to the end of the Cold War. It concludes by discussing whether and to what extent these strategies may help the OSCE to overcome its current crisis.

Asymmetric bargaining

The comprehensive agenda of the CSCE was not established by design. Rather, it was a product of tough bargaining over the possible outcomes of the Conference, with the East and the West pursuing contentious visions and preferences.[7]

The Soviet Union aimed to ratify the territorial and political status quo in Europe that had taken shape after World War II. It sought a pan-European conference to replace the Final Settlement with Respect to Germany and to consolidate its sphere of influence within the Yalta order. For this purpose, Moscow prioritized reaching agreement on a set of principles governing inter-state relations and emphasized the inviolability of frontiers. The Soviet bloc also added economic and environmental co-operation to its initial agenda proposal.

Particularly in the United States, this policy was viewed as "compatible with a key premise of Nixon-Kissinger foreign policy," which proceeded on the basis that the status quo "was the only realistic policy compatible with American interests."[8] However, the 1969–1971 debates within NATO revealed that West European governments, while open to discussing principles, favored expanding the agenda by including issues such as the freer movement of people and ideas and militarily relevant confidence-building measures. They also sought to resolve practical humanitarian cases and to include respect for human rights and fundamental freedoms in the catalogue of principles. Having accepted the principle of the inviolability of frontiers in the 1970 treaties with Moscow and Warsaw, the Federal Republic of Germany sought to leave the door open for German reunification by emphasizing the possibility of a peaceful change of borders.[9] After several months of resistance at the 1972–1973 preparatory consultations for the CSCE, the Soviet Union accepted this extension of the agenda.[10] This shaped the three baskets of the CSCE: security-related issues (principles and confidence-building measures); economic and environmental co-operation; and humanitarian co-operation, including human contacts and information exchanges.

As a result of protracted negotiations, the 1975 Helsinki Final Act was based on a myriad of trade-offs within and between the individual baskets. The most notable of these included balancing the principle of the inviolability of frontiers with the clause on the peaceful change of borders that was added to the text of the principle of sovereign equality, the inclusion of the human rights principle in the Helsinki Decalogue, and specific provisions pertaining to human contacts and information exchange. These trade-offs framed the balance of the Helsinki Accords, which each party considered sufficient to justify accepting the overall outcome of the negotiations.

The Conference benefitted from the asymmetric preferences of the participating States, as this meant that each of them had a stake in the agreement. The agreement did not do away with the asymmetry itself, however, which was manifested in the participating States' different assessments of the CSCE outcomes. The Soviet Union and its allies emphasized the inviolability of frontiers (while silencing the peaceful change clause) and, later, non-intervention in domestic affairs. Both principles were believed to have ratified the territorial and political status quo in Europe. In the West, by contrast, emphasis was put on the dynamic provisions of the Final Act, primarily on those included in the humanitarian third basket (as well as on the peaceful change clause) and, later, on the human rights principle. These provisions were meant to support the idea that the Helsinki trade-offs were an agreement on a modus vivendi that allowed for change in the future. Both the East and the West believed that time was working in their favor.

The open nature of the Helsinki process and uncertainty regarding where it would ultimately lead fed criticism both in the West and in the East. Different preferences remained at the core of East-West disputes at the subsequent follow-up meetings pertaining to both the implementation of the Helsinki provisions and next steps to be agreed upon.

The process

Critics of the Final Act in the West argued that the commitments on which the East and the West had agreed were imbalanced. They maintained that the Final Act mainly benefited the Soviet bloc, pointing to the differences between the reversible and the irreversible commitments into which the East and the West had entered. In particular, they stressed that the Soviet bloc had achieved its main goal by endorsing the inviolability of borders in Europe (an irreversible commitment). At the same time, provisions concerning the freer flow of people and ideas across the East-West divide had yet to be implemented, making the West dependent on the goodwill of the East (and thus making this a reversible commitment). It was hoped that this could be remedied by conceiving of the CSCE as a process rather than a single event and by reaching agreement on a series of follow-up meetings that would discuss, *inter alia*, the implementation of the Helsinki Accords.

Unsurprisingly, the East and the West diverged on this issue. It was the Soviet Union that had proposed the institutionalization of the CSCE at the beginning of the Conference. However, it lost interest in this proposal as the provisions of the third basket of the Final Act began to take shape. At the end of the negotiations, Moscow was prepared to limit the Conference to the signing of the Final Act. The West, by contrast, having initially been hesitant to consider the institutionalization of the CSCE, was increasingly interested in a follow-up process that would make it possible to reconfirm, implement, and improve its dynamic commitments. The respective provisions of the Final Act, although limited to the determination that the first follow-up meeting would open in Belgrade in 1977, were instrumental to shaping the Helsinki process. The follow-up meetings were to serve three major purposes in particular: to ensure the continuity of the CSCE process, to hold participating States accountable for implementing the relevant CSCE commitments, and to discuss further proposals for developing CSCE commitments.

The Belgrade Meeting largely failed to achieve these goals. After the election of Jimmy Carter as president, the United States emphasized human rights and pushed for the implementation of the relevant provisions of the Final Act. Instead of proceeding with quiet diplomacy, the new administration did this in a very public way. The Soviet Union arrived in Belgrade with a wide (largely declaratory) disarmament agenda and proposals for launching ambitious pan-European economic projects. While the United States showed little interest in discussing disarmament and was concerned that the extension of the CSCE agenda in this direction would distract attention from human rights, the Soviet Union dismissed this approach as shifting the balance of the Helsinki process. It clearly communicated its reluctance to enter any new commitments in the third basket, sought to shield itself from publicly discussing its human rights record in an international setting, and emphasized the principle of non-intervention in domestic affairs. A number of European participating States attempted to identify common ground by showing interest in discussing the economic projects proposed by Moscow in exchange for some improvement in the human dimension, but this ultimately failed. As a result, the Belgrade Meeting fell short of producing a substantive outcome, although it secured the continuation of the CSCE process by agreeing to schedule a second follow-up meeting, to open in Madrid in 1980.

A flexible agenda and balanced progress

One lesson from the Belgrade Meeting was that balancing the asymmetric interests of key stakeholders was a major challenge for the Helsinki process. This was not limited to the debate over the implementation of previously reached agreements, which was subject to divergent interpretations by various participating States. Rather, redefining the balance of interest at every stage of the process could facilitate the implementation of earlier accords as part of new trade-offs.

This gradually led to a recognition of the need to ensure balanced parallel progress in the different baskets of the Helsinki Final Act, most notably ensuring that progress in the human dimension matched that in the security field (and vice versa). Three circumstantial factors contributed to this approach in the 1980s. First, the Conference's agenda was never rigid. Although the participating States agreed on a specific list of issues to be addressed when negotiating the Final Act, nothing in the rules of procedure precluded them from expanding this agenda after 1975 (should they decide to do so by consensus). Of course, this did not imply that the CSCE would deal with everything the participating States wished to put on the agenda. In 1972–1973, during the preparatory consultations, the general understanding was that the CSCE would concentrate on issues that were relevant to East-West relations. The participants opposed putting the Middle East conflict on the agenda, despite strong advocacy by the then Austrian chancellor Bruno Kreisky. The only exception was the addition of a modest Mediterranean dimension to the CSCE in response to pressure from the prime minister of Malta, Dom Mintoff. Second, after the Belgrade Meeting there was a process of rethinking the US strategy, which led to the recognition that the confrontation over human rights was becoming counterproductive and did not facilitate the implementation of the Helsinki Accords. Indeed, after some liberalization in the mid-1970s, the Soviet policy on human contacts and the dissemination of information hardened once again.[11] Third, France (from 1978) and the Soviet bloc (from 1979) pursued parallel proposals for convening a Conference on Disarmament in Europe (CDE). Their visions for the CDE gradually converged, but both pursued the CDE proposal outside the CSCE as an autonomous project.

Although the United States' attitude toward a disarmament conference was ambiguous to say the least, growing support for the French initiative among its European allies led Washington to appreciate the value of expanding the security agenda of the CSCE. This was even more so since the French (and later the Soviet) proposal anticipated holding the CDE in two stages. It reduced the mandate of the first stage of the CDE to discussing further confidence-building measures should progress be made in the human dimension of the CSCE. The consideration of disarmament measures would thus be postponed to the second stage, if and when it were agreed upon. In discussions within NATO, the United States encouraged France to submit the proposal within the CSCE at the Madrid Meeting rather than pursuing it as a separate project. Although the Soviet Union rejected the direct linking of security and human rights issues, by the opening of the Madrid Meeting it gradually moved towards accepting the principle of balanced parallel progress in all areas of security and co-operation in Europe.[12]

Beginning with the Madrid Meeting, further development of the CSCE was based on balancing the progress reached in the field of security with that in the human dimension. Although East-West relations were extremely tense in the early 1980s, the Madrid Meeting adopted the mandate of the CSCE Conference on Confidence- and Security-Building Measures and Disarmament in Europe scheduled to open in Stockholm in 1984. This decision was balanced by a number of new commitments in the human dimension, as well as the decision to convene two meetings of experts: one on human rights (Ottawa, 1985) and one on human contacts (Bern, 1986). Progress in both dimensions—security and human rights—was to be assessed at the third follow-up meeting in Vienna, which was scheduled to open in 1986. Western states made moving to stage two of the Stockholm Conference conditional on substantial progress in the human dimension.[13] Although the continuation of negotiations on security issues within and outside the CSCE after the Vienna follow-up involved many complex issues, the United States would keep an eye on retaining a "security lever" in the Helsinki process, as otherwise Soviet co-operation could not be expected.[14]

Elaborating on commitments

As a result of multiple trade-offs, many commitments included in the Helsinki Final Act were formulated in a general way and/or in ambiguous terms. Apart from this, many caveats, particularly in the third basket, provided room for interpretation. This triggered controversies at the follow-up meetings regarding the interpretation and implementation of specific provisions. Many proposals put forward at these meetings were therefore aimed less at breaking new ground than at spelling out the more general Helsinki commitments in greater detail to reduce ambiguity and to limit the scope for interpretation, thus making their implementation verifiable.

Consider the following example. The Helsinki Final Act called on the participating States to "*favourably* consider applications for travel" for the purposes of facilitating human contacts.[15] The modest easing of restrictions on private travel abroad reported by the Soviet Union and other Soviet bloc states at the subsequent follow-up meetings was criticized by some in the West as an inappropriate implementation of the respective commitment in the Final Act. Following the implementation debate and the submission of the relevant proposals, the Concluding Document of the Madrid Meeting specified that "favourable consideration" meant that decisions on such applications for the purposes of family reunification and marriage between citizens of different states would be made "in normal practice within six months."[16] In the 1989 Concluding Document of the Vienna Meeting, commitments related to facilitating human contacts were elaborated in great detail; in particular, it was specified that applications for the purposes of family meetings were to be decided within one month "in normal practice," and applications for the purposes of family reunification or marriage within three.[17]

Of course, the pace of this process was far from impressive, much like the pace of the Helsinki process as a whole, which required great patience. However, the specification of the controversial provisions of the CSCE documents made the commitments clearer and verifiable. The Vienna Follow-up Meeting—concluded fourteen years after the signing of the Helsinki Final Act—put an end to controversies related to implementing the humanitarian clauses of the Final Act.

Conclusions and recommendations

How much of the CSCE experience remains a part of history, and how much remains relevant to the OSCE today? Following recent debates within the Organization, CSCE veterans must be experiencing a strong sense of déjà vu. Criticism from Russia and other participating States regarding thematic imbalances in the Organization's operations—its excessive focus on the human dimension at the expense of security issues[18]—reveals a clear asymmetry of preferences similar to that found within the CSCE. This suggests that if and when the participating States resume dialogue on restoring the European security order, asymmetric bargaining will likely be their mode of negotiation.

Prior to the war in Ukraine, the search for a new trade-off was supposed to be informed by seeking reconciliation between Russia's commitment to the indivisibility of security and freedom of alliance, rather than between the inviolability of frontiers and the West's emphasis on the possibility of their peaceful alteration.[19] This will certainly change after the war. Although the agenda will largely reflect its yet unknown outcome, the issue of borders in Europe will likely remain on the agenda for the foreseeable future. Until we can expect a lasting settlement of the current conflict, the eventual trade-off is likely to involve agreeing on a set of rules for managing a modus vivendi rather than establishing a new status quo. While such rules cannot simply reconfirm the existing normative basis of the OSCE, they could build on it while introducing relevant adjustments—for instance by further specifying the principle of non-intervention in domestic affairs or provisions related to the freedom of the media and the free dissemination of information—in order to reduce the scope for interpretation. These adjustments would have to be negotiated by the participating States, although the relevant OSCE structures could facilitate the process.

Should the OSCE, as a result of the current crisis, return to its Cold War roots and be reduced to a venue for political dialogue,[20] the concept of balanced progress in different dimensions could again have relevance. If and when dialogue on the future of the European security order resumes, the OSCE could be a natural platform, given its inclusive membership. It would benefit from the existence of permanent structures and institutions that would prevent it from being terminated abruptly should the participating States fail to agree on the next follow-up meeting.

However, the role of the OSCE as a platform for dialogue should not be taken for granted. While the Soviet Union acted as a *demandeur* that was ready to make concessions during the Helsinki negotiations and process, Russia has resisted resuming such a role. Over the past fifteen years, when seeking a settlement with the West, Russia has explicitly avoided using the OSCE as a venue for such discussions. The 2008 Medvedev proposal for a European Security Treaty was pursued by Moscow outside the OSCE, and in early 2022, during the short discussion of Russian security guarantees, Moscow's clear preference was to pursue this discussion with the United States and NATO rather than the OSCE.[21] Nevertheless, insofar as dialogue on European security cannot be limited solely to the OSCE and would be conducted in multiple settings, the future role, shape, and operations of the OSCE may well be subject to a broader trade-off.

Notes

1 John J. Maresca, *Helsinki Revisited: A Key U.S. Negotiator's Memoirs on the Development of the CSCE into the OSCE* (Stuttgart: ibidem-Verlag, 2016), 38.

2 Yuri Vladimirovich Dubinin, "Ambassador Yuri Vladimirovich Dubinin of the Soviet Union," in *CSCE Testimonies: Causes and Consequences of the Helsinki Final Act 1972–1989*, CSCE Oral History Project (Prague: Prague Office of the OSCE Secretariat, 2013), 214–16. Until 1989, subsequent follow-up meetings were to determine the venue and the opening date for the next meeting. In case of failure to do so, the CSCE process would be discontinued.

3 Victor-Yves Ghebali, *The Diplomacy of Détente: The CSCE from Helsinki to Vienna* (Bern: The Library Am Guisanplatz BiG, 2019), 23.

4 Andrei Zagorski, *Хельсинкский процесс. Переговоры в рамках Совещания по безопасности и сотрудничеству в Европе 1972–1991* [The Helsinki process: Negotiations within the framework of the Conference on Security and Co-operation in Europe 1972–1991] (Moscow: Prava Cheloveka, 2005), 153.

5 Zagorski, cited above (Note 4), 172.

6 William Korey, *The Promises We Keep: Human Rights, the Helsinki Process, and American Foreign Policy* (New York: St. Martin's Press, in association with the Institute for EastWest Studies, 1993), 179–80, 214–15.

7 See, for instance, Markku Reimaa, *Helsinki Catch: European Security Accords 1975* (Helsinki: Edita, 2008); Andreas Wenger, Vojtech Mastny, and Christian Nünlist, eds., *Origins of the European Security System: The Helsinki Process Revisited, 1965–1975* (London: Routledge, 2008); Zagorski, cited above (Note 4), 31–114.

8 James E. Goodby, "The Politics of the Helsinki Process: How Did It Arise During the Cold War? An American Perspective," in *Peace and Prosperity in Northeast Asia: Exploring the European Experience* (Seogwipo City: JPI Press, 2008), 1:124.

9 Goodby, cited above (Note 8); Christian Nünlist, "Helsinki+40 in the Historical Context," *Security and Human Rights* 25, no. 2 (2014): 201; Zagorski, cited above (Note 4), 31–44.

10 Zagorski, cited above (Note 4), 53–54.

11 Korey, cited above (Note 6), 101, 115.

12 John Borawski, *From the Atlantic to the Urals: Negotiating Arms Control at the Stockholm Conference* (Washington: Pergamon-Brassey's International Defense Publishers, 1988), 19–25; Zagorski, cited above (Note 4), 157–61.

13 One outcome of this development was the 1989–1990 negotiation on conventional forces in Europe by the NATO and Warsaw Pact member states "within the framework" of the CSCE that led to the signing of the CFE Treaty.

14 Borawski, cited above (Note 12), 133.

15 CSCE, Conference on Security and Co-operation in Europe Final Act (Helsinki: 1975), 39, https://www.osce.org/files/f/documents/5/c/39501.pdf, emphasis added.

16 CSCE, Concluding Document of the Madrid Meeting 1980 of Representatives of the Participating States of the Conference on Security and Co-operation in Europe, Held on the Basis of the Provisions of the Final Act Relating to the Follow-Up to the Conference (Madrid: 1983), 19, https://www.osce.org/files/f/documents/9/d/40871.pdf

17 CSCE, Concluding Document of the Vienna Meeting 1986 of Representatives of the Participating States of the Conference on Security and Co-operation in Europe, Held on the Basis of the Provisions of the Final Act Relating to the Follow-Up to the Conference (Vienna: 1989), 25–29, https://www.osce.org/files/f/documents/a/7/40881.pdf

18 Andrei Zagorski, "Russia and the OSCE," in *OSCE Insights*, Special Issue, eds. Frank Evers and Argyro Kartsonaki (Baden-Baden: Nomos, 2022).

19 Zagorski, cited above (Note 18).

20 See, for instance, Matthias Dembinski and Hans-Joachim Spanger, “Pluralistic Peace: New Perspectives for the OSCE?,” in *OSCE Insights*, ed. IFSH (Baden-Baden: Nomos, 2022), 173–83.

21 The Ministry of Foreign Affairs of the Russian Federation, “Foreign Minister Sergey Lavrov’s Remarks and Answers to Media Questions at the Joint News Conference with Following Talks OSCE Chairman-in-Office, Minister of Foreign Affairs of Poland Zbigniew Rau, Moscow, February 15, 2022,” February 15, 2022, https://mid.ru/en/foreign_policy/news/1798511/

Why the OSCE's Forum Function Matters

Jelena Cupać[*]

Abstract

This contribution examines how participating States can better use the OSCE's forum function. Drawing on lessons from other international organizations and the historical evolution of the CSCE/OSCE, the paper offers recommendations on how participating States can use this function to de-escalate tensions and to prepare for the future. The focus is on how to dissuade Russia from thinking that its goals can be achieved through violence while still incentivizing it to stay engaged in the OSCE.

Keywords

International forum, OSCE, Ukraine, Russia, war

To cite this publication: Jelena Cupać, "Why the OSCE's Forum Function Matters," in *OSCE Insights*, eds. Cornelius Friesendorf and Argyro Kartsonaki (Baden-Baden: Nomos, 2023), https://doi.org/10.5771/9783748933625-07

Introduction

The all-out Russian invasion of Ukraine in February 2022 has caused an existential crisis for the OSCE. The problem is not only that the Organization lacks the capacity to sanction Russia for violating core OSCE principles but also that the war has exacerbated existing difficulties, such as agreeing on the OSCE's budget. Commentators and practitioners therefore wonder whether the Organization can overcome such enormous pressure and, if so, in what form. One frequently mentioned option is reducing the OSCE to its forum function, which, some observers hope, would facilitate state co-operation and dialogue.[1] It is still unclear whether the OSCE will develop in this direction or whether it will be able to maintain its other organizational functions. Nevertheless, one thing seems likely: if the Organization survives, its forum function will become ever more important as participating States seek to cope with the situation in Ukraine.

This paper discusses the forum function of international organizations (IOs) and offers recommendations on how OSCE participating States can use it constructively. It first discusses the forum function as encountered in other IOs. It then takes a closer look at its evolution

* Jelena Cupać
WZB Berlin Social Science Center
jelena.cupac@wzb.eu

in the case of the CSCE/OSCE, observing how it has changed along with geostrategic shifts in Europe. The final section makes recommendations on how participating States can use the OSCE to dissuade Russia from thinking it can achieve its goals through violence while simultaneously incentivizing it to remain engaged in the Organization. It also recommends using the OSCE's forum function for deeper engagement with the Western Balkans, the South Caucasus, and Central Asian countries in planning the future of European security.

International organizations as forums

The forum function is the most basic function of IOs. IO forums serve as meeting places for states to discuss their interests and decide on matters of mutual concern.[2] A defining characteristic of international forums is their openness and inclusiveness; each state is allowed to express its interests and preferences on a given topic. Although decision-making rules in forums vary across issue areas, security IOs are more likely to decide by consensus and unanimity.[3] The result of such decision-making is that decisions often reflect the lowest common denominator. As much as they are places for state co-operation, forums can also be places of fierce confrontation. Nevertheless, this does not diminish their role as a multilateral environment for de-escalation, socialization, and trust-building.

The forum function is a part of both formal and informal IOs. Informal IOs, such as the G20 and BRICS, are effectively just forums. They do not have headquarters or permanent bureaucracies and are built on the non-committal engagement of states. As for formal international organizations, most of their state-based bodies can be described as international forums. However, since some of these bodies have restrictive membership and decision-making procedures, plenary meetings (such as the UN General Assembly) are usually seen as the primary site of the organizational forum function.

States use forums to achieve specific purposes. These purposes vary across IOs and depend mainly on the problem area in which the IO and its forum are active. An economic forum will have a different purpose than a public health forum. For security organizations such as the OSCE, the central purpose pursued by participating States is peace. How states communicate their preferences and interests within an IO and the value they attribute to that IO change over time. To understand how participating States could use the OSCE forum constructively amid the war against Ukraine, it is thus helpful to look to history.

The changing purpose of the OSCE's forum function

The OSCE's predecessor, the Conference on Security and Co-operation in Europe (CSCE), was a state forum *par excellence*. It emerged against the background of the Cold War; following the 1962 Cuban Missile Crisis, the United States and the USSR agreed to open lines of communication to ensure peace and stability. In the following decade, this shift opened the way to US-Soviet détente: a general willingness to pursue peace by relaxing tensions, including through strategic arms limitations. At the same time, through its *Ostpolitik*, West Germany sought to normalize relations with Eastern Europe, particularly with East Germany. The CSCE's Helsinki Final Act resulted from the confluence of these trends.[4]

The Act was not only the result of the superpowers' willingness to negotiate. More important was their acceptance that, at that historical moment, peace in Europe could only be pursued through a recognition of the status quo rather than a stubborn desire to change it. The Helsinki Final Act was thus an expression of the pursuit of so-called "plural peace": peace among states who recognize each other's normative differences and the geostrategic reality such differences have created.[5] The Act was considered a significant victory for the Soviet Union as it allowed it to fulfill its long-standing goal: the West's recognition of its postwar hegemony in Eastern Europe. On the other hand, the West could use it to criticize the Eastern bloc for its human rights violations. In this way, the participating States reached a modus vivendi, which would keep the door open for future changes.

Following the end of the Cold War, the CSCE transformed into an international organization, albeit one without legal status. It was rapidly institutionalized, with its forum function transferred to state-based bodies: the Permanent Council, the Parliamentary Assembly, the Ministerial Council, and the Summits. However, the purpose of these forums changed substantially compared to the Cold War years. Participating States no longer used them to pursue plural peace. Instead, they focused on building "liberal peace": peace based on the co-operation of states dedicated to liberal democratic values. In a succession of documents adopted in the early 1990s, they thus established that human rights could flourish only in pluralistic democracies,[6] that only orders composed of democratic states can be truly peaceful,[7] that human rights violations should be a matter of legitimate concern to all participating States,[8] and that such violations represent root causes of conflict.[9] On this basis, the OSCE established specialized bodies and dispatched field operations to facilitate and supervise democratization processes across the former Eastern bloc.

This liberal peace phase of the OSCE did not last long. Soon after NATO announced in 1994 that it expected and would welcome expansion,[10] the forum bodies of the OSCE became arenas of confrontation, with states using the Organization's normative catalog as a resource for justifying individual interests. The West used them to continue to push for the liberal vision of peace, insisting that most violations in the OSCE area were happening in the human dimension and that participating States had the sovereign right to choose or change their security arrangements, including treaties and alliances. By contrast, Russia insisted that NATO's expansion violated the politico-military dimension, particularly the principle of indivisible security. At the same time, it began to object to the OSCE's democracy-facilitating bodies, portraying them as interfering in the internal affairs of states for the sake of Western geostrategic goals. Consequently, for nearly three decades, the OSCE largely hobbled along as a confrontational forum, with its field operations, democracy-facilitating bodies, and politico-military instruments frequently falling short of their stated purpose.

This brief historical overview shows that the CSCE/OSCE's forum function has constantly changed in response to changes in European security. While it was initially intended to establish peace between blocs of states with different regime types, its purpose then shifted to building liberal democratic peace. It now remains divided between these opposing perspectives. Against this background, this paper offers recommendations on how the OSCE might be used as a forum for keeping participating States engaged, enabling them to de-escalate tensions and to prepare for the future. These recommendations consist of communicating clear boundaries to Russia in the politico-military dimension while making limited concessions in the human dimension.

Discussion and recommendations

Normative messaging and signaling

In the short term, the OSCE forum function will likely stay on roughly the same course it has been on for nearly three decades. The participating States will continue to use the Organization and its principles and commitments to point out each other's violations and offer justifications for their own actions. In other words, they will continue to use the OSCE as a forum for communicating the boundaries of what they view as an acceptable security architecture in Europe. In the context of the war against Ukraine, however, Western states have an opportunity to give new meaning to this long-standing blame game. Along with economic sanctions and military aid to Ukraine, they could use the OSCE to put Russia under additional pressure by engaging in the practice of "normative deterrence": that is, they could send Russia a clear and resolute message that under no circumstances will they compromise on OSCE principles. In particular, the West could communicate to Russia that it will not engage in negotiations on zones of influence or discuss European security in similarly retrograde terms, including if Russia succeeds in keeping parts of Ukraine under prolonged occupation.

In short, the OSCE could be used in these new circumstances to continuously remind Russia that the Decalogue's principles, including the inviolability of frontiers and the territorial integrity of states, are firmly established and will not be subject to renegotiation. From this perspective, the principal goal of "normative deterrence" would be to discourage Russia from believing it can achieve its aims through violence and to prevent such behavior from becoming an accepted precedent.

Keeping Russia engaged

In their pursuit of normative deterrence, Western states should be careful not to marginalize Russia entirely. After all, Russia's sense of marginalization amid the EU's and NATO's eastward enlargement may have played a role in its decision to use violence against Ukraine. Therefore, in addition to using the OSCE to increase normative pressure on Russia in the politico-military dimension, Western states should look for ways to keep the country engaged, in the hope that such engagement will allow them to rebuild trust and de-escalate hostilities in the years to come.

One way of doing so would be to give Russia a sense that the OSCE's liberal aspirations have diminished. The Russian leadership has long seen these aspirations as a threat rather than a solution to lasting peace in Europe. It has often portrayed the work of OSCE institutions dedicated to the values of democracy and human rights as part of a Western strategy for interfering in participating States' internal affairs, sometimes aimed at regime change. Therefore, an OSCE with a strong liberal purpose is likely to attract more criticism than engagement from the Putin administration.

Knowing this, Western states could strategically tone down their rhetoric on human rights and democracy for the time being. This does not mean giving up on liberal norms. Western states can continue to reaffirm their strong commitment to human rights and democracy, thus keeping them a vital part of the OSCE's normative repertoire. But they could also recognize that such reaffirmation does not have to go hand in hand with using these norms to blame and shame Russia and other authoritarian participating States, a practice that has often played into their fear of regime change.

The advantage of this approach is that it would not go so far as to recognize Russia's authoritarian regime as an equal and legitimate interlocutor in European security (a status that was granted to the Soviet Union via the Helsinki process). It would also not go so far as to introduce a principle of inviolability of domestic political orders, given that such a move might embolden rather than discourage Russia in the context of the war in Ukraine.[11] Yet it would still be an important step in preventing Russia's further alienation, as it would relieve at least some of its anxieties about the OSCE's being a Western tool for regime change. This approach might allow participating States to build a reserve of trust and to use that trust to de-escalate hostilities and seek co-operation in areas of mutual concern.

Planning the future

In addition to deterring and engaging Russia, Western states could also use the OSCE's forum function to prepare for the future. This could be done by seeking deeper engagement with participating States that are neither EU nor NATO members. While most of these states are connected to the two IOs through various arrangements (such as accession negotiations, the Eastern Partnership, the Enhanced Partnership and Cooperation Agreement, and the Partnership for Peace), the OSCE remains the only multilateral security arrangement that brings them and the West under one roof. Most of these states belong to the Western Balkans, the South Caucasus, and Central Asia—regions that have traditionally been vulnerable to Russian influence. Due to energy and other dependencies, some of them have been reluctant to condemn Russia's invasion of Ukraine. Loosening security ties with these regions might bring them under more significant Russian influence, inflame their longstanding conflicts, or boost their authoritarian tendencies. Western states should therefore use the OSCE's forum function to deepen security relations with these regions and, aware of all current and future difficulties, invite them to jointly shape European security.

Notes

1 Matthias Dembinski and Hans-Joachim Spanger, "Pluralistic Peace: New Perspectives for the OSCE?," in *OSCE Insights*, ed. IFSH (Baden-Baden: Nomos, 2022); Jos Boonstra, "The OSCE: Back to Square One?," in *Russia's War Against Ukraine: Implications for the Future of the OSCE*, OSCE Network Perspectives I/2022, eds. Cornelius Friesendorf and Stefan Wolff (OSCE Network of Think Tanks and Academic Institutions, June 2022), 14–17.

2 Ian Hurd, "Theorizing International Organizations: Choices and Methods in the Study of International Organizations," *Journal of International Organizations Studies* 2, no. 2 (2011): 7–22; Robert O. Keohane, *After Hegemony: Cooperation and Discord in the World Political Economy*, 2nd ed. (Palo Alto: Princeton University Press, 2005).

3 Daniel J. Blake and Autumn Lockwood Payton, "Balancing Design Objectives: Analyzing New Data on Voting Rules in Intergovernmental Organizations," *Review of International Organizations* 10, no. 3 (2015): 377–402.

4 David J. Galbreath, *The Organization for Security and Co-operation in Europe (OSCE)* (Abingdon, UK: Routledge, 2007).

5 For more on plural peace, see Dembinski and Spanger, cited above (Note 1).

6 CSCE, Document of the Copenhagen Meeting of the Conference on the Human Dimension of the CSCE (Copenhagen: June 29, 1990), https://www.osce.org/files/f/documents/9/c/14304.pdf

7 CSCE, Charter of Paris for a New Europe (Paris: November 19–21, 1990), https://www.osce.org/files/f/documents/0/6/39516.pdf

8 CSCE, Document of the Moscow Meeting of the Conference on the Human Dimension of the CSCE (Moscow: October 3, 1991), https://www.osce.org/files/f/documents/2/3/14310.pdf

9 CSCE, Second Meeting of the Council, Summary of Conclusions (Prague: January 30–31, 1992), https://www.osce.org/files/f/documents/7/b/40270.pdf

10 Ministerial Meeting of the North Atlantic Council/North Atlantic Cooperation Council, Partnership for Peace: Invitation Document (NATO Headquarters Brussels: January 10–11, 1994), https://www.nato.int/cps/en/natohq/official_texts_24468.htm

11 Markus Kaim, Hanns W. Maull, and Kirsten Westphal, "The Pan-European Order at the Crossroads: Three Principles for a New Beginning," SWP Comments 18, March 20, 2015, https://www.swp-berlin.org/en/publication/new-pan-european-order

Zeitfracht Medien GmbH
Ferdinand-Jühlke-Straße 7
99095 Erfurt, Deutschland
produktsicherheit@kolibri360.de